Moral Imagination

Moral Imagination

A Decision-Making Process for Individuals and Organizations

Catherine L. Sommervold

ROWMAN & LITTLEFIELD
Lanham • Boulder • New York • London

Published by Rowman & Littlefield
An imprint of The Rowman & Littlefield Publishing Group, Inc.
4501 Forbes Boulevard, Suite 200, Lanham, Maryland 20706
www.rowman.com

86-90 Paul Street, London EC2A 4NE

British Library Cataloguing in Publication Information Available

Library of Congress Cataloging-in-Publication Data

Names: Sommervold, Catherine, 1969- author.
Title: Moral imagination : a decision-making process for individuals and
    organizations / Catherine Sommervold.
Description: Lanham : Rowman & Littlefield Publishers, 2021. | Includes
    bibliographical references.
Identifiers: LCCN 2021032097 (print) | LCCN 2021032098 (ebook) | ISBN
    9781475860122 (cloth) | ISBN 9781475860139 (paperback) | ISBN
    9781475860146 (ebook)
Subjects: LCSH: Decision making. | Creative ability. | Hope.
Classification: LCC BF448 .S66 2021 (print) | LCC BF448 (ebook) | DDC
    153.8/3—dc23
LC record available at https://lccn.loc.gov/2021032097
LC ebook record available at https://lccn.loc.gov/2021032098

For J, C, M, and J, and all those trying to make a difference.

A man, to be greatly good, must imagine intensely and comprehensively; he must put himself in the place of another and of many others. . . . The great instrument of moral good is the imagination.

—Percy Bysshe Shelley, *A Defense of Poetry*

Contents

Preface

As this edit of the book wraps up, it is December 2020. It has been quite a year, to say the least. The year 2020 was not anticipated and has changed the way individuals, industries, and organizations operate.

Floods, fires, epidemics, pandemics, protests, riots, and highly contested and aggressive elections led to isolation, fear, business closures, and working remotely or through hybrid models for schools and countless other organizations. Some states banned gathering with anyone living outside of the host's home to celebrate the holidays.

While each individual responded to these circumstances differently, it is a fact that everyone was impacted. There was no longer "business as usual." People now speak of the "new normal."

This is the perfect time for this book. The process of moral imagination helps people arrive at creative solutions and make sound long-term decisions in the face of circumstances that have never before been experienced. It is a way to move forward without a map.

Moral imagination as a decision-making process helps individuals and organizations make better personal and professional decisions. It provides upcoming leaders with a process that allows them to propose creative solutions to problems.

Imagination and creativity are key components of hope. It is time for a decision-making process that embraces hope and builds in the space to reflect on past events and find new ways to build what needs to happen. As a species, we humans have collective memory and intelligence;

when we combine these collaborative efforts with moral imagination, we can create solutions that are, as yet, undreamed.

Be well. Wash your hands.

Introduction

Everyone makes decisions—every day. The good news is, everyone can make good decisions. The magic question then becomes, How does one know when one is making good decisions? What is a good decision anyway? Good decisions are creative, empathetic, and long term. A good decision provides a solution that aims to create the best possible situation for everyone involved. In order to make good decisions, one must take into account what events transpired to create the current circumstance, examine past patterns and circumstances, and identify stakeholders and personal biases.

Welcome to decision-making with moral imagination. The process outlined in this book will provide readers with a concrete process to make good decisions.

This process facilitates good decisions. It allows decision makers to communicate their conclusions and the process they followed to reach those conclusions. When a clear understanding of the process to reach a decision is communicated, confidence in the decision maker increases. A shared understanding of the decision-making process is an example of transparency, which leads to trust.

Many leaders do not know how to begin or what things to consider when making a choice. They "go with their gut," which works . . . until it doesn't. This book is based on research, best-practice decision-making, and centuries of reflection about moral imagination; it provides a tried-and-true path to sound decisions.

Good ideas are classic and timeless. A good idea has wisdom. It is approachable and honest, and it resonates. A good idea works regardless of context and climate. Decision-making with moral imagination is a good idea. It encourages creativity and innovation. It is a process that actually facilitates gathering all the information and creating a best-possible outcome. It can work with design thinking, first- or second-order changes, or any other models of brainstorming and strategic planning.

It is also a decision-making safety net. Problem-solving and creating solutions need to be objective and tied to the components of the situation that one is trying to resolve rather than subjective and prone to the whim of the person in charge. Even in cases when decision makers may have questionable moral compasses, this process creates an outcome that considers important necessary components and protects the interests of those involved. Crazy, right? Moral imagination is what the world needs.

But . . . *moral imagination*? What does that even mean? There are strong central components that emerge as common within the descriptions or characteristics of moral imagination. These components are brought forward and become the key points that create a process that can be followed to make decisions that are morally sound and, because of the extent of the process, can be transparent and easily communicated by decision makers.

In its truest form, moral imagination is the process of utilizing imagination to more effectively sort through the pieces that impact making sound, creative decisions. The creative component of moral imagination allows decision makers to actively imagine a solution that has never been utilized before, that may work where something else has not worked. The use of the words *moral* and *imagination* does not mean that decision makers get to use their moral compass and imagine what they decide is right. They do not get to create whatever and deem it ok.

For some, the term *imagination* conjures images of fairy dust and unicorns; this is not what it is. Imagination is different from *imaginary*. The imaginary is something that is conjured and can only exist in the mind. The imagination is involved in using past information to predict or determine what may happen in the future.

As an example, the fanciful creations of children and their imaginations create things that do not and could not exist, such as unicorns and hufflelumps. Imagination is different. The unicorns and the solution to answering the question, "What should I wear today?" all come from the same process. This is a distinction that is important to the rest of this book.

We often refer to the imagination as a thing people do or do not have, but actually, imagination is a process. When people say, "She has a great imagination," they are actually saying, "She uses her imagination well and has good ideas [either real or imaginary]." This occurs much in the same way as when someone says, "She is a great artist." The speaker actually means, "She is a creative person who has good ideas and paints [or writes or sculpts or sings or cooks or weaves or ...] well."

Imagination takes the old and familiar and, through reflection and revision of experience, creates something new. Imagining is a necessary facility to take what has been known and to predict what is unknown but may become known. Imagination can be used to solve real problems and to create real solutions. Imagination is used daily. Even those who claim to have no imagination use it daily, starting with something as simple as deciding what to wear.

Picture this: An alarm goes off; an arm stretches lazily over to the bedside table and picks up a phone; a set of eyes pry open, look at the phone, and turn off the alarm. The phone is set back on the bedside table, and the body flops back into bed. Eyes stare at the ceiling and the mind races as the to-do list for the day is reviewed.

1. First use of imagination: nothing is being done. No one is looking at a list. Instead, the brain is being used to access prior and familiar events to predict what will happen today. As the list is completed, a yawn erupts. Then a stretch. A hand picks up the phone to check the weather. Sixty percent chance of rain.
2. Second use of imagination: as the possibility of rain is considered, prior information is accessed, and the imagination is used to retrieve experiences in similar circumstances and make a prediction about what should be brought and worn. Again, this is accessing the use of imagination; it is allowing one to think about what it may be like outside, and how it feels to be wet, and then to choose to bring an umbrella, wear a raincoat, or dance in the rain.

Imagination is critical to the function of daily life. It is the process by which prior knowledge and information about a situation—the emotions, past responses, points of view of those involved, and so forth—are used to create (predict/answer) a response to what is unknown. In some instances, imagination is used to envision next steps; those next steps can involve a response to the weather, a response to someone receiving either good or bad news, or even the solution to a more serious problem.

Moral imagination is an imaginative process in that it draws on the imagination of the decision maker not to make things up or be fanciful but to access empathy and visualize long- and short-term, intended—and possibly unintended—consequences. To make a good decision, a decision maker must *imagine* what might happen, how someone might feel, or how something may respond.

Moral imagination is a moral process in that it seeks the best solution when two or more solutions could be right or wrong, when none of the choices is clearly the best option. It is moral in that it helps address a dilemma. Dilemmas are difficult decisions with no clear right answers. An example may be a situation that puts the rights of the individual up against the rights of the community. A decision to make an allowance for one employee may make the community as a whole feel undermined. There are valid arguments on both sides about which rights are more valuable.

Moral imagination, as a process, helps the decision maker through a series of steps and creates empathetic solutions in situations where there may not be clear answers. It leads to decisions that are sound. This is important, especially now. This book provides an outline of the process of moral imagination and in doing so, presents it as a tool that can help leaders feel more confident and work toward a consistent process for decision-making and a way to work toward the best possible solutions.

This is a necessity. Research about how leaders make decisions indicates that most leaders do not have consistent decision-making processes. Most leaders, such as college presidents, executive directors, superintendents, principals, and CEOs—people who have careers leading and deciding—cannot articulate the steps they take when they make decisions. If the people who make decisions for a career do not have a clear process, it is easy to conclude that this information is necessary for everyone.

Time should be taken to demonstrate how to make sound decisions. People need to be shown which important things to consider and how to transfer that information; without these steps, the decision-making process may not be well thought through. People do not have a consistent process for making decisions, nor do they approach problems in the same way. Good decision-making and the processes involved in making good decisions must be explicitly taught and modeled.

Leadership classes cover types of leadership, organizational dynamics, strategic planning and goal setting, and how to analyze budgets, but most programs do not teach leaders how make and articulate decisions. Leaders need to be trained to reflect on and dissect past decisions to see what transpired. Work with leaders and doctoral candidates clearly shows that this area needs more focus during instruction. The shortsighted, narrow decision-making paradigms of the past need to evolve. The process presented here is that evolution.

This book is the result of an assumption. A newbie researcher assumed good leaders made good decisions and *knew how they did it*. When it became clear that this was not actually the case, the next logical step was to see how things actually exist in practice. Leaders who made decisions on a regular basis were asked how they went about the process. The result was that there was no consistency in outcome or approach. Best-practice decision-making literature helped clarify these results.

Not surprisingly, when good decisions are made, both best-practice decision-making and the components of moral imagination are present. These pieces—best-practice decision-making and the components of moral imagination—overlap and support each other. With this in mind, this book combines the components of moral imagination and best-practice decision-making to outline an evolved process for decision-making. Examples and hints about how to use the process to make the best choices are included.

Educators and researchers who would consider a review of the literature on this topic to be important may find it as an appendix following the references at the back of the book. As such, all the academic pieces of the book are in a single place. Those who just want to get to the heart of the information, who are most interested in getting to the meat of how to use this process to make better decisions, may just want to take note that the review is included, should they ever need it.

Chapter One

A Journey to a Process

This chapter will discuss how the moral imagination process was refined, and it includes the twenty-thousand-foot view of how moral imagination, as a process, came to be. The introduction references a review of literature. The presence of a review of literature indicates that the history of moral imagination is largely philosophic. Curiosity about how moral imagination overlapped with best-practice decision-making pushed toward the evolution of a process.

Moral imagination is the ability to imagine which antecedents created a problem, how the various constituencies involved in the problem may view the events, and how the various consequences and outcomes might unfold. The process of moral imagination in decision-making increases the thoughtfulness of the decision.

The use of imagination requires creating images of what could be and therefore involves the consideration of possible consequences. In application, identification of the process of moral imagination should indicate thoughtful decision-making as evidenced by examining antecedents, considering multiple perspectives, and imagining possible consequences of the available outcomes. There are decided points researchers can look toward to determine whether moral imagination is being used. These points can be operationalized and utilized as the process of moral imagination

The term *moral imagination* has been around for ages. There is a theoretical evolution as well as sporadic (but persistent) references to moral imagination made by pundits and philosophers across centuries and from all philosophic backgrounds (see the appendix). In a time when so much seems polarized, this idea has historic support from all sides of the political compass. Not in spite of but because of this polarization, the concept of moral imagination is as relevant today as it was in the 1700s.

The term *moral imagination* is present in mainstream print, social media, and television. Almost a decade ago, President Obama urged Americans "to expand our moral imaginations, to listen to each other more carefully" and to "remind ourselves of all the ways that our hopes and dreams are bound together." This was in response to the tragic deaths of six individuals following a shooting at the University of Arizona.

In 2019, Obama used this term again in describing the work of the late Toni Morrison: "Toni Morrison was a national treasure, as good a storyteller, as captivating, in person as she was on the page. . . . Her writing was a beautiful, meaningful challenge to our conscience and our moral imagination. What a gift to breathe the same air as her, if only for a while."

Senator Cory Booker, a 2020 Democratic presidential hopeful, used the term to describe a way to think of policies differently and to counter the idea that things need to be realistic: "I am also somebody who says we need to expand the moral imagination in this country of what's possible."

In these references, *moral imagination* is a noun phrase. It is a reference to a changing morality. It is something a person possesses and uses—like a bicycle.

The problem with interpreting moral imagination as a possession is that it alludes to the idea that one either has moral imagination or one does not. In the examples above, there is focus on moral imagination as almost a synonym for conscience and a determination of right from wrong. While this is definitely a part of this process, there is so much more.

Human minds are vast, and their ability is untapped. No matter the problem that humans encounter, we will always find a better solution if we approach it correctly. This is positive. As technology and critical thinking gurus noted at the turn of this century, "We are educating students for jobs that do not yet exist." It's no different now, which, rather than causing alarm, should be seen as hopeful.

As the 2020 political and medical climates have demonstrated, there is no longer a set road map for how to school, how to do business, or how to make decisions. And this is ok, because so many past decision-making models are obviously biased, having been created to serve a specific goal. While deference has been paid to empires, countries, and ideologies, and particular generations had their moment in history, none of these any longer holds the best and future interests of our emerging population in the highest regard.

There are current pieces of the way problems are solved and solutions are conceptualized that would do well to crumble into the abyss. If that happened, there would need to be a new way to involve more voices and lift up new ideas. Thought leaders have an obligation to explicitly provide instruction and models for problem-solving that are moral, creative, and imaginative.

As each individual is allowed to chart an unknown course toward career and purpose, there must also be a new way to make decisions. A decision-making process that takes new information into consideration, imagines the best possible solutions, and strives for those solutions is required. Moral imagination is this process. It allows individuals to work together and demonstrate a way to solve problems that is forward thinking. The use of moral imagination as a process simultaneously provides structure and flexibility.

A few things to remember:

1. This is a process. It can be started at any point of the process.
2. All parts of the process must be completed for it to actually work.
3. When the process is mastered, it goes faster; reflecting on prior knowledge to access pieces rather than reinventing the wheel can happen.

The process of moral imagination:

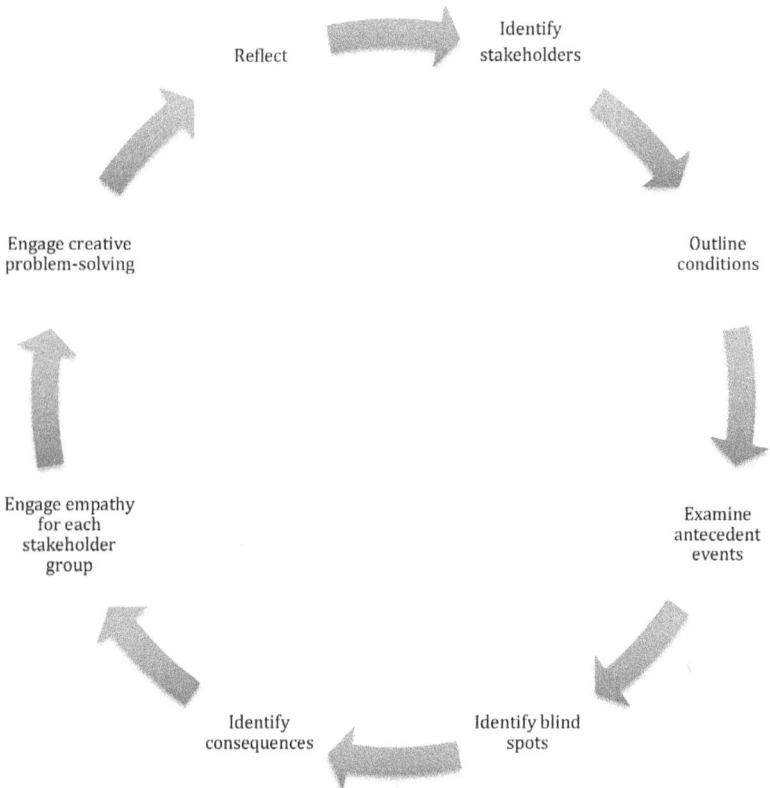

Figure 1.1. Moral Imagination Process
Sommervold Dissertation, 2010.

So where to begin? As indicated, this process can be started at any point, but most leaders, when faced with a tough decision, usually start with an analysis of the problem to be solved. As Albert Einstein said, "If I had an hour to solve a problem, I'd spend fifty-five minutes thinking about the problem and five minutes thinking about solutions."

One of the first points to recognize about this process is that it involves not only the decision maker but also other people. These people, who are referred to as stakeholders, must be considered with regard to their opinions and possible responses to intended and unintended consequences.

It is also important to acknowledge that leaders are persons with faults. All individuals have things they may overlook or error toward, which are referred to as blind spots. A blind spot may consist of forgetting to include a stakeholder group or perspective. A blind spot may also be always having a bias toward something.

While the process under discussion shares many components with other best-practice decision-making models, in order to be considered the moral imagination process, several distinct components need to be evident. A process is a series of steps taken in order to achieve a particular end. In this case, the end reflects a look outside the obvious; it is the futuristic consideration of possible consequences, which include empathy and respect for antecedent events.

The component parts of moral imagination are:

Stakeholders
Conditions
Antecedent Events
Blind Spots
Consequences
Empathy
Creative Solutions
Reflection

This process provides a framework for effectively executing decision-making and is a tool to analyze and critically examine past decisions. Decisions that have had poor outcomes missed adhering to one or more steps in the process of moral imagination. Decision-making is easier when there are distinct steps to follow. When past decisions are analyzed and the places that are most likely to be overlooked or undervalued in the decision-making process are evaluated, this information can be used to make adjustments and correct for past mistakes.   I n this age of moral consciousness, a time when many fear making a judgment because they do not want to risk causing offense, how do we effectively lead and learn to discern the best choice? When all business, leadership, political, and academic decisions ought to be moral, the task can be daunting. Using the process of moral imagination to develop creative answers is the answer to this question.

The process of moral imagination to make decisions is used successfully in a variety of capacities. It is used to help not-for-profit organizations clarify directions so they can begin strategic planning. It helps leaders make decisions and analyze where decision-making processes broke down in the past. It is even used each fall by many doctoral students as an analysis tool in their introduction to doctoral studies course.

The careful consideration and deliberation used in making decisions with moral imagination is not necessary when making an easy decision. Easy decisions are decisions that have obvious right and wrong answers. In contrast to easy decisions, moral decisions are messy. Moral decisions often have several answers that may be considered right and therefore can also be considered wrong. This process gives decision makers a framework to sort through the messiness of challenging decisions.

The more conscientious leaders are, the more aware they are that validity may exist on all sides of a decision. It is the tension in choosing between ends that makes a situation difficult. In the act of deciding, one chooses between one thing and another; while this process is quite common, there are times when the results are more complex.

Every day a person makes decisions: whether to get up or stay in bed, whether to go to work or stay home, or whether to eat or skip breakfast. Some of these decisions are easy and straightforward, and others are moral in that they cause conflict and the need to hesitate and consider options before taking action. Decisions dictate our days, and the results of these decisions—both intended and unintended—direct our actions.

Individuals in leadership positions tend to make decisions that will impact more people than themselves. Whether it is a head of family making a decision to change jobs or a community leader making a decision to change boundaries, the consequences of decisions can have far-reaching implications. Corporate leaders make decisions that impact employees, consumers, and, therefore, the economy. Political leaders make decisions that may impact our laws or our personal freedoms. Educational leaders make decisions that may impact themselves, their immediate staff, and the generations of learners who depend on the systems they lead.

Moral imagination is a process that includes imagining what created a problem, how those involved in the problem may view the events, and how the various consequences and outcomes may unfold. In both near and distant futures, the process of moral imagination in decision-making increases the thoughtfulness of the decision. The process is becoming relevant on a national stage.

Patricia Werhane, Wicklander Chair in Business Ethics and the director of the Institute for Business and Professional Ethics, echoes this: "Moral imagination is a necessary ingredient in management decision-making. Otherwise, one often gets trapped in a particular 'schema' or narrative that fails to take into account important dimensions of one's activities. This entrapment may lead to difficulties or even disasters" (Werhane, 1999). "Individuals who exercise moral imagination, including the ability for discerning moral issues and developing a range of possible outcomes during the decision making process, are indeed more likely to generate a mutually beneficial outcome for a situation compared to those who do not" (Godwin, 2008).

Leaders need to move beyond the comfort of past paradigms and imagine a future of solutions that integrate the huge number of perspectives a complex decision contains. Participation in the process of moral imagination allows for this type of futuristic problem-solving. This can only happen if leaders imagine an ideal solution and strive for it. This quest to create what is right is moral.

Individuals in leadership positions need to make decisions that are mutually beneficial; in order to do that in a dynamic twenty-first century, leaders need to be able to imagine unique moral solutions. A quotation attributed to Albert Einstein applies here: "We can't solve problems by using the same kind of thinking we used when we created them" (Einstein and Calaprice et al., 2010). This ingenious note provides a clear bridge from the past schema to a future of moral imagination that is beneficial and indicative of a sound, reflective decision-making process.

Chapter Two

What Are the Parts?

How Do They Fit Together?

The component parts of moral imagination listed in the previous chapter have distinct roles in the process of decision-making. This chapter provides a more detailed description of each component in the moral imagination process and briefly describes how to approach using the process. A person can actually jump into the process at any point. It is best, when faced with a tough decision, to start with an analysis of the problem to be solved.

Once the problem is determined, this process follows a series of steps in order to achieve a particular end. Each of these steps will be examined in individual chapters, which also include examples of how the step is important to help leaders navigate challenging decisions. Once the problem has been identified, the steps of the moral imagination process are:

- a careful consideration of the decision maker's blind spots
- a thorough understanding of the situation at hand, including the consideration of all stakeholders and the events that led to the dilemma
- a reflection upon what has been done (both by the leaders and relative to the decision at hand) and an identification of where things may have gone more smoothly
- a proposal of a creative solution
- a prediction of both long- and short-term intended and unintended consequences of proposed solutions

- an empathetic understanding how each of the consequences would impact stakeholder groups
- creative futuristic problem-solving

The components of moral imagination are:

Stakeholders
Antecedent Events
Conditions
Empathy
Blind Spots
Consequences
Reflection
Creative Solutions

The first three components—conditions, stakeholders, and antecedent events—deal with adequately defining and understanding the context in which the decision rests. These steps consider who is involved, what the setting is, and what led to the point of this tough choice.

The next three components—empathy, blind spots, and consequences—are related to understanding the influences and emotions that impact the decision. Finally, consequences, reflection, and creative solutions all deal with understanding the options from which to choose and the intended and unintended implications of each of those choices.

In an ideal world, decision makers would begin the process of decision-making with a few concrete steps: reflect on their past experiences, examine their blind spots, and infer who has been affected by the decision in the past, how they have been affected, and who will be affected in the future. Decision makers would then use their imaginative capacity to put themselves in the shoes of the stakeholders and envision how these antecedent events unfolded. How do things look from all sides of the current situation?

At this point the decision makers would again engage their imaginative capacity and through these multiple stakeholder lenses envision the possible outcomes and consequences of the current situation. They would use their imagination to make predictions dependent on which solution they opted to choose. Finally, they would construct alternate and creative solutions. Leaders who take all of these background things

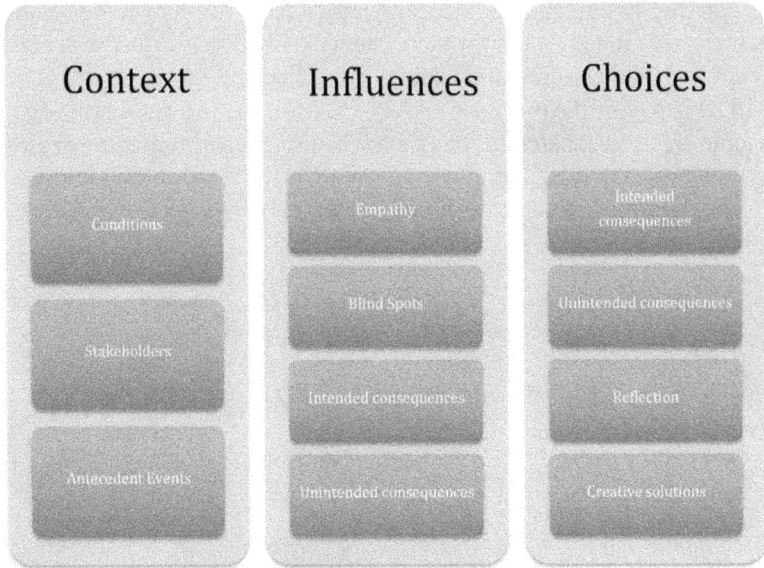

Figure 2.1. Three Components of Moral Imagination
Sommervold Dissertation, 2010.

into consideration and construct a unique solution are utilizing moral imagination.

This process is important culturally as well as practically. More than two decades into the twenty-first century, the idea that we are creating learners to solve problems that do not even exist is still alive and well. As the lines between business and personal life become further blurred by the inclusion of personal electronic devices, Zoom meetings, and the new work-from-home paradigms, the ethical implications of our choices touch more things.

Decades ago, if a banker made a bad decision at work, his family might never know what had happened. Similarly, if a college president made a business deal that was a potential conflict of interest, it might take years to sort out. Now all decisions have the capacity to be immediately public and scrutinized. This immediacy increases the need for transparent decision-making.

Leaders know that they can never make everyone happy. If a choice is made that pleases one group, it is most likely going to alienate, if not aggravate, another. No process will ever alleviate that problem, but a leader who has a concrete and complete process for making decisions is more able to transparently and systematically discuss what was considered. While research and experience demonstrate that not everyone will be happy, if the process of how a choice is made can be explained, people are at least placated. In a time when so many people have explosive and visceral reactions to what is going on in the world, this is a win.

The steps that make up the process of moral imagination are a cyclic, not linear, process.

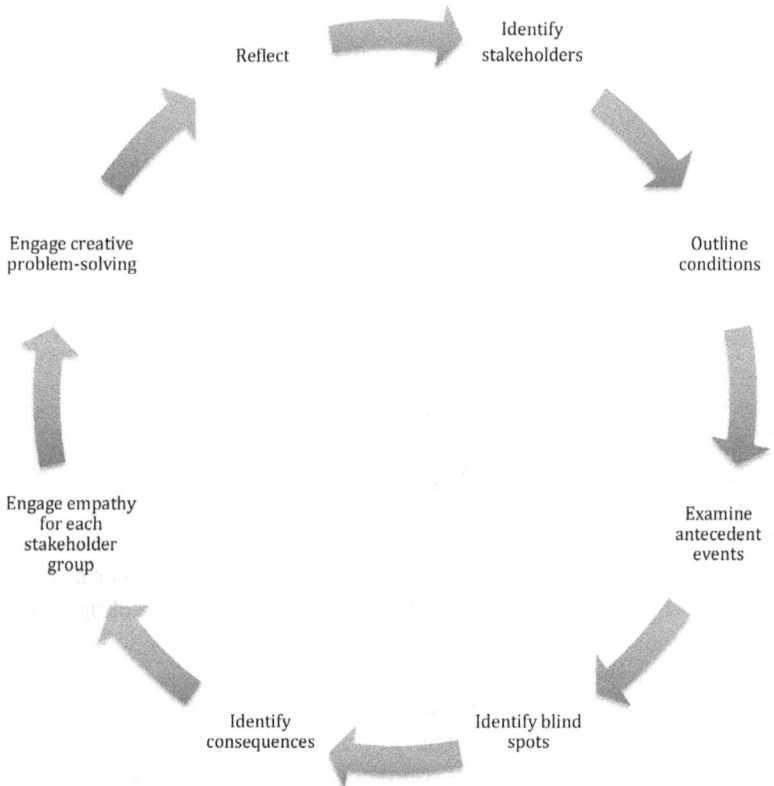

Figure 2.2.   Moral Imagination Process
Sommervold Dissertation, 2010.

There is no step 1, step 2, step 3, and so on. People jump into this process at any point. As an example, leaders may find themselves mid-reflection and realize that they have forgotten to include an important stakeholder group in their consideration of the decision. Leaders just need to include the groups that they have missed and continue to work through the other steps of the process. Each step is important, and all of the steps must be included for the process to be complete, but the order in which they are completed is not relevant.

Chapter Three

Stakeholders

While the identification of blind spots is dependent on the decision maker, the identification of stakeholders is decision dependent and may change as the circumstances surrounding an event change. The first component in the process of moral imagination that will be addressed is the identification of all of the stakeholders involved in a decision. A stakeholder is someone who has an interest in the decision that is being made or, more specifically, in the outcome of a decision that is being made. Identifying stakeholders is one of the three fact-finding/background research pieces of the moral imagination process.

The distinction when identifying stakeholders in the moral imagination process, as opposed to other processes, is that when a decision is challenging, the stakeholder list needs to be exhaustive. One of the most common mistakes made by decision makers is that they make decisions in isolation. The inclusion of stakeholders and the subsequent solicitation of stakeholder opinions counteract the effects of isolation. When a leader is compelled by process to make a list of all who may be impacted by a decision, consider how each of those groups may feel about the decision, and even move to the point of asking some stakeholders for their opinions, decisions are not made in silos.

While important, this step is not complicated. In fact, identifying stakeholders is very straightforward. A decision maker must sit down and make a list of everyone who may be impacted by the decision being made. It is that simple, but remember: the list needs to include everyone. When decision-making mistakes have been in the realm of stakeholder consideration, it is often that all groups involved in a situation are not identified or that the viewpoints of certain groups are actually omitted.

There are several examples of the omission of stakeholder considerations creating problems. In the first example, during an interview with a community college president, when asked to name the stakeholder groups associated with a decision to move the location of the campus, the president made a long list including community and board members. But, consistent with his decision-making, he never once mentioned the adult students he served.

The students did not make it into the stakeholder group, and it was evident in the way this president made decisions that he did not consider their opinions in the factors that influenced his decision-making process. As a result, the decisions this president made did not benefit and, actually, negatively impacted the students. When this oversight was pointed out to him, his only response was, "Oh. I guess I should have included them."

In another example, fifty years ago the governor of a small midwestern state was very progressive. This governor saw that computers would change the ways schools operated and students learned. He pledged that all of the schools in his state would have computers, and in unanimous support, the legislature approved the expenditure. While this grand gesture had noble intentions, the governor and his staff failed to consider the people impacted most directly by the decision to purchase computers.

If anyone had asked, administrators and teachers in the schools of the state would have mentioned important things like the lack of infrastructure and the lack of understanding the staff of the schools had for computers. As a result, much money and time were wasted, as decades later, state staff would visit schools to find computers, still in boxes, dusty, and stacked in the corner of classrooms, never opened because no one knew what to do with them.

In each of these examples, if the decision maker had thought through the stakeholder groups and included or even gone so far as to solicit their opinions, resources and relationships could have been preserved.

There are times when giving careful consideration to everyone involved in a situation is beneficial. When asked to share an example of a decision that went well, a superintendent of a midsize school district shared the decision-making that was involved in building a new school.

This superintendent credited the inclusion of all stakeholders from elderly community members to the students to the custodial crew for making this process successful. To his credit, this leader understood that to have changes go smoothly, one needed the support and cooperation of all involved parties.

Stakeholder inclusion builds trust and gets people invested in the process. In order to obtain buy-in, to borrow a word from corporate literature, all the involved parties need to feel as though they have a vested interest in the initiative at hand.

In the case of the superintendent referenced above, he did his background research and knew that often local bond initiatives fail because community members who do not have school-age children fail to understand the value a new school brings to the community. When this group of stakeholders was questioned about their concerns, those concerns were addressed; as a result, those without children in the community saw the value a new school would bring, and they fully supported and even petitioned for the effort.

The superintendent in this example had the sole goal of doing what was best for the students. As a result of this goal, he took time to consider whom the students saw each day and who made a difference in the lives of the students. There were many obvious answers—teachers, aides, lunch ladies—and one uncommon answer: the custodial staff.

The superintendent watched the interactions in his school buildings. He saw that often the custodians were the first and/or the last people to greet students and that when the custodians were happy with how things were going, they helped things go more smoothly for everyone else. At first, the custodial staff seemed neutral regarding the construction of a new building, but wanting their input and buy-in, the superintendent asked their opinion regarding building materials and storage areas.

He learned that the custodians did not like carpet, as when something was spilled on it, it was hard to effectively clean without a steamer. Carpets were removed from the design plan, and the custodians had a vested interest in the new buildings. The custodians cared for the facility as if it were their own and welcomed and supported those who entered the buildings more graciously than they had previously.

It is important to consider everyone involved or impacted by a decision that is made. It may not be necessary to speak to each individual involved, but, on some level or another, there is a need to answer to all of them. When it is obvious that individuals' opinions have been considered, the inclusion of their opinion and the consideration of their point of view will increase their support and investment in the outcome of the decision a leader makes.

When a leader takes time to consider all of the stakeholder groups, it is easier to communicate to the groups how and why a decision is ultimately made. It is obvious that the importance of each group is recognized. While people often shy away at first when they are asked for their opinions, it is still important. It is important for each group to be identified and able to effectively address its concerns.

Chapter Four

Conditions

An important fact-gathering step in the moral imagination process is an understanding of the conditions surrounding a decision. Conditions are the facts: the context of the decision. In what state is one located? At what time of year does the decision take place? The easiest way to think about the conditions of a decision is to think of them as the setting of the decision.

If a decision were a book, the conditions would be the time of year, geographic location, political location, century, decade, weather . . . any of these. A decision looks different in a company of five people in rural South Dakota than it might in a company of three thousand in Manhattan, New York.

An example that illustrates how understanding the condition of a decision has an impact on the process of moral imagination and decision-making is what one might do in a situation when an employee is found with marijuana in her system. An employee was out with friends and used marijuana in her leisure time. Nothing went awry, the employee was not arrested, but someone identified her on social media as using recreational THC and reported her.

What should a boss do in this situation? It depends. This situation looks vastly different in 2020, depending on the state in which the employee resides. Outside of any guidelines within a contract or employee handbook, there are several states that have legalized the use of marijuana for both recreational and behavioral use. The setting of this dilemma can greatly impact the outcome.

A less dramatic example is that of an eighth-grade class who have all been in the same rooms since they were in kindergarten. After years of having comparable standardized test scores, this year they have vastly different scores. Neither teachers, nor administrators, nor area education agency workers could figure out what could cause this discrepancy.

A look at the conditions surrounding the test taking indicated that one half of the class took the test before lunch and the other half took it after lunch. The class that took the test after lunch did not finish as much of the test and did not do as well. This is all easily explainable: historically, students are tired and sluggish after lunch. An examination of the conditions indicated the cause of the issue.

On a larger scale, the year or decade may factor into a condition to be considered. The racial tension of 2020 looks very different from that of 1920. It may not always be the case, but our location and timing impact things more than often than we care to admit. A careful description and accounting of the conditions helps decision makers make more thoughtful choices. Be sure to understand the conditions of the situation, in order to have a better understanding of how the choices play out in the end.

Chapter Five

Antecedent Events

In order to truly understand what is happening, a leader must first understand what transpired prior. One must ask, "What events unfolded to create this situation?" Remember that dear Albert Einstein was spending those fifty-five minutes thinking about the problem prior to the five minutes thinking about solutions. Examining the antecedent events, also known as the background events or what caused the situation, is another critical step in thoroughly understanding the problem.

Identification of the antecedent events to a dilemma is one of the three fact-finding steps in the moral imagination process. In addition to identifying stakeholders, the people impacted by a potential decision, it is important to examine how the current situation came to be. Remember, the process of moral imagination is necessary only in decisions that are dilemmas: situations in which there are no clear right or wrong answers. In many situations, solutions become clearer when the road that has been traveled becomes clear.

A word of caution: the examination of antecedent events can send one down a rabbit hole. A person must go back far enough in the history of a situation to understand what the biases and tensions are between the sides of an issue, while being careful not to go back so far as to examine how Pangaea was formed. The goal in identifying antecedent events is to determine the history of the current dilemma of one's organization and, if people are divided among ends, to try to determine what has influenced people in choosing the sides they have chosen.

The research of past events may or may not need to go back to legislative acts or even to the influential years of the adults involved, but identifying the chain of decisions and interactions that led to a difficult choice is important. There are times when the antecedents are obvious and historical, as in the case of residents of a local Native American reservation being hesitant to trust or take at their word white people who come in and try to work with students.

Antecedent events may be subtle or culturally specific to a building or organization. An easy example of this occurred when a new director came into a local arts organization and saw that the staff was awful: they were rude, they arrived late and left early, and they did not provide good customer service. The only conclusion the new director made was that she was going to have let them go and bring in new staff.

When the director shared with her board the idea of letting the staff, the board told her in no uncertain terms that she would not be able to let them go. The reason the organization hired a new director was that it had come to the attention of the board that the old director had not been doing his job for quite some time. The current staff had been enthusiastic and willing to work when they started, but under the negligence and apathy of the old director, they had never received training and had lost their passion for the organization.

The board asked the director to wait, work with the staff, and determine if she could help them fit into the organization before helping them find another place to succeed. Had the director sought the antecedent events before getting frustrated, she would have learned about the attitude of the past director and been able to work with the staff in a more timely fashion.

Information about the course to the current situation is not always readily available. While the best and easiest method to getting information regarding the antecedent events of a situation is to just ask the people involved, this is one of several methods. The three main ways to gather information regarding antecedent events are through examining archival records, interviewing or having conversations with stakeholders, and soliciting the help of key cultural guides within an organization.

In order to discover antecedent events through archival information, any piece of evidence can be examined—for example, old newspaper articles, agendas, or board meeting minutes. More realistically, in this day and age, much of this information is most likely online and can be searched there.

The trick is to remember to get both sides (or all sides, if there are more than two) and go back far enough to learn about how a situation began. As pointed out earlier, it is most likely the case that there are both large historic issues and more nuanced cultural issues at play; be sure to develop a solid understanding of both. If a search engine fails, there is always the option to look to other online sources and scroll through social media.

The following example illustrates how easy this can be and what an impact it can make. In one midwestern state, donation buckets were being passed at all high school football games to raise funds to support an injured quarterback. Buckets were being passed at games in all districts except one. The obstinate district was named West Pine. When asked if the buckets could be passed in his stadium during the next game, the West Pine superintendent had to hesitate and do some homework before agreeing.

This is where antecedent events—background events, as they were— become so interesting. The superintendent hesitated because early in his career, in a different state, he had let someone pass the hat for donations and neglected to ask the appropriate questions. Unfortunately, the hat was passed for a cause that was very political, and it had turned out to be controversial.

Antecedent events can be as useful for the person presenting the question as they are to the decision maker. If the person making the request had learned more about the history of the West Pine superintendent, the person could have provided more details and the superintendent might have agreed sooner.

This all ended well. The superintendent made a call to a colleague and then got online to find out all football games in the state were collecting funds for a young quarterback who had sustained a head injury and was in a medically induced coma. The superintendent agreed to collect donations in his stadium as well.

When looking for interviews, the best strategy is for one to ask people if one can sit down with them and ask them a few questions. It is easier to ask people how they feel about a situation, how they believe a situation reached the point of dilemma, and what they believe could be done to remedy a situation, than to guess.

Visiting with people works best if the stakeholders are identified first. Best practice is to find a couple of examples in each stakeholder group and ask their opinion. This also creates buy-in. People are more likely to support a decision if they feel their opinion was taken into consideration.

If organizing a time to ask questions in an actual interview-style setting seems too complicated and intimidating, have informal conversations. Seek people out in groups or individually at a ball game or community event and ask their thoughts.

Research on focus groups indicates that people are often more honest when they are not in a one-on-one situation with someone, so it may be best to find several members of a stakeholder group together and ask their thoughts. While it is always best to ask people how they feel about things, as situations become more complex, this can become time-consuming and may cause conflicts.

It is also possible to find someone with organizational memory—that is, the cultural guide of the organization. Find the person who knows why it is bad to move the photocopier or how to tell if the union contracts are going to get negotiated. Often this can be a receptionist, administrative assistant, or even a long-time member of the board or a parent organization.

One can often identify who the person is, make time to sit down with the person, and ask the questions one needs answered about how the current situation came to be. Remember to get all sides of a story to the extent it is possible. If possible, get to the root: ask questions to see why things played out the way they did.

Any one of the above methods or a combination of them will be helful in gathering the information to put together the sequence of events that led to the current dilemma. Look locally and nationally; often a little bit of both has influenced what is happening.

Chapter Six

Blind Spots

One of the most challenging things to ask of decision makers is that they focus their attention on themselves. A critical step in the process of moral imagination is to identify the personal blind spots of a leader. Identifying blind spots requires decision makers to turn the magnifying glasses on themselves. During this step in the process, it is necessary to take deliberate steps to identify personal shortfalls and biases.

On an individual basis, identifying blind spots means taking a moment to consider personal biases in decision-making: the good, the bad, and the ugly. What things does the leader take for granted? What things are good? What things does the leader favor though the leader may not even be willing to admit it out loud? Make sure the list is thorough. It may be surprising.

In some instances, what may need to be done will require going all the way back and examining things that were family beliefs that may not obviously impact decision-making but could do so indirectly. Think back to dinner-table discussions that helped form opinions of what was good or bad, who was a hero or a villain, or who needed help and by whom. The following is a good example.

My family history is one of independent businesspeople. While I was growing up, my father ran the third generation of the family business. I bring this up because at first glance, this fact is harmless. Good for them! Supporting the economy is good. Family business is good. Independent business owners are the American dream incarnate.

The question becomes, Is this relevant to how I make decisions? If so, how? As it turns out, this is quite relevant. This fact is, I came to discover the basis for one of my blind spots. One of the unspoken beliefs of the independent businesspeople I knew was that it was better to be struggling and be in control of one's own time and destiny than to have to answer to anyone else.

How does this translate to a blind spot? Professionally, it became a blind spot, because for many years, I was embarrassed that I was not my own boss. I unfairly elevated those who were and would give preference to those who took that risk and were willing to be "in control" of their destinies. A person would have to work very hard to convince me that someone who was trying to start a business—any business—wasn't a little bit of a hero.

This impacted my decision-making because, right or wrong, I supported and made decisions that were by conventional terms a little risky. These pieces from dinner-table discussions led me to struggle personally with the fact that I was a professor and researcher—respectable by most standards but hard to accept because I had a supervisor or two.

An example in education is that of an assistant superintendent. He reviewed several decisions he had made during the course of an interview. Some decisions went well; some didn't go so well. It was only after reviewing a choice he made to change a bus route so it could pick up a particular child and deliver said child to school that he sat silently.

The assistant superintendent said, "I didn't think I had a blind spot. I do. I definitely do. I will always defer to the underdog. The child who has less. I will always work for that child, even when it isn't fair to other children, because I believe that child should have someone in her corner. I was that child, and I didn't have anyone in my corner, and I wished I had."

The assistant superintendent chose to have other students stay on a bus longer and change the bus route to go outside of boundaries so one particular child could get on the bus and get to school. This may be the right choice because it demonstrates empathy for the child. It may be the wrong choice because he was unfair to the other children on the bus and a bus route should not be changed for one person. Regardless, his blind spot heavily influenced how he decided.

It makes sense to identify blind spots when making decisions. It is a good idea to do it before decisions need to be made. It is, however, one of the small things people often do not take the time to do. It is hard to know how to start.

It is often easier to look for blind spots by first trying to do so with past decisions. Is there a pattern in the way decisions were made? Is there a consistent social justice bent? Is there support for the status quo? Are rules always followed explicitly?

Examining what has been done in the past can help identify patterns and determine which factors were influential in order to predict how decisions may be made in the future. This identification allows a decision maker to either support trends and continue to make decisions the same way *or* take steps to make sure blind spots are not causing judgment errors.

In deliberating a challenging decision, a leader should start the process by gauging gut impressions. What are the various sides of the dilemma? How have those been determined? When the decision comes to pass, the leader should ask, "Regardless of what is right, what is not being seen that may impact decision-making?"

As in the examples that were shared, the blind spot could be the result of something from childhood. It could be something that happened last week. It could be that a leader of an organization unfairly burdened one area of staff over the other and may be making decisions that try to mitigate that fact—thereby overcompensating. What things are impacting how the stakeholders are seen and what outcomes are desired?

After asking these questions and reflecting on past actions, leaders may be able to convince themselves that they are objective decision makers, that they do not have a blind spot. At this point, it would be safe to counter that idea. The idea that anyone is so objective as to not have a blind spot combined with overconfidence in the one's own decision-making ability may, in fact, be a blind spot.

All of this may sound very obvious, but it becomes evident that people rarely take this point into account when, after decisions have gone poorly, they use this one step as an analysis tool to begin to evaluate what went wrong. There may be a number of reasons that this happens. When asked why they do not use a consistent process for making decisions, many leaders default to the idea that it takes too long.

Some may think it takes too long to spend a few minutes defining how they feel about the pieces of a decision and what biases they have relative to those. It may be that considering blind spots is difficult because individuals are hesitant to focus a spotlight on themselves. Many leaders, especially those in helping fields, are hesitant to spend time on themselves.

The most obvious reason is that, because they are blind spots, a leader just may not see them. The good news is that once someone has taken the time to outline blind spots, this reflection does not need to happen every time a difficult choice is made other than for trying to predict how they may impact a current situation.

Failure to identify blind spots can create problems in the process of decision-making that impacts the choices that are made. Consequences for failing to identify blind spots may unfold for a leader who cannot articulate why a decision was made.

Not being able to explain how a choice is made may not sound like a big deal, but it can be. It can impact the buy-in and support of followers and team members, it may cause decisions to be made inconsistently and decrease leadership credibility, or, in a worst-case scenario, it may cause decisions to be made by feel rather than by logic and cloud a leaders' ability to see which organizational problems they may actually be causing.

The failure to identify blind spots occurs in organizations and systems in much the same way it occurs in individuals. Just as an individual leader may have a bias toward or away from helping one group or another, so do organizations and systems. As an example, many would say that the current state of our national penal system reflects bias. Some would say the lack of inclusion of politically diverse opinions on college campuses indicates a bias in academia.

From an input-output standpoint, systems create exactly the product they are designed to create. If one's system, one's organization, is not producing what it should, an organizational blind spot may be causing the issues. While many organizations identify their explicit biases openly in the form of mission and values statements, the blind spots that can negatively impact decision-making are often the implicit or subtle biases or cultural norms that unwittingly impact decisions.

As an example, a volunteer advisory board in a smaller metropolitan area stated that it was very interested in increasing availability and accessibility to the nonmajority groups in the area. While it was not tied to the mission of the organization, an increase in diversity would definitely expand its reach and vision (and is always a good idea). The board had always been dominated by Midwest corporate CEOs and professional volunteers because the makeup of the community been largely homogenous.

When it was suggested that the best way to incorporate voices that had not traditionally been heard was to offer board positions to community members who had not traditionally been involved and had more diverse backgrounds, the board nodded, agreed, and then never acted upon the idea. While everyone involved would be horrified to admit it, there was an unspoken racial bias within the organization, and that bias led to making community decisions that did not represent all aspects of the community.

What follows is a final example of an organizational blind spot. It is not uncommon for organizations that mean well, that exist to lift another out of untenable situations, to arrive on with solutions in hand. When an external organization comes in with a solution to a problem without visiting with those whom it serves, the implication is that the people "in need" are not smart enough to come up with a solution on their own.

Organizations historically enter into a group of underserved or underrepresented adults presuming that the group doesn't know what should be done instead of recognizing that the group lacks the resources to begin or that there may be another impediment to creating a solution, with or without the aid of an outside organization.

The blind spot here is the belief that the group of underrepresented adults does not have a solution. This is an example of the "logical" conclusion of the helping organization. It is assumed that because nothing has been done, the group could not solve the problem. In the following example, let us look at a bias against Native American reservations.

Organizations swoop in and dictate solutions, because there is an organizational (or even cultural) blind spot that the people on the reservations do not have solutions. This bias distracts from the process of effectively working toward a solution, engaging the moral imagination, and creatively solving existing problems, because while it not only operates from a blind spot, it is also condescending.

Even the process of taking time to recognize that organizational blind spots exist can help eliminate short-term miscommunications and allow people who have the same goal to work together more effectively. The identification of blind spots can be used to help analyze what has gone wrong in past situations. Repeatedly, decisions that have produced underside or poor outcomes have been the result of decisions being impacted by blind spots.

Chapter Seven

Empathy

Empathy, along with prediction of consequences, is one of the two components of moral imagination that most heavily rely on imagination. This chapter will discuss empathy and its importance in the moral imagination process. Empathy is the capacity to imagine what someone else is feeling—to be able to so closely imagine what someone else is feeling that one can feel it or conjure a time one felt the same way.

The idea that empathy is important to decision-making and, in fact, to life in general is not new. Philosophically, the role empathy plays in decision-making and in creating a socially just world cannot be downplayed. Consider this: if children cannot use their imagination to create a representation of something with which they are most likely familiar, like a kitten but without a kitten in front of them, it is unlikely they can pretend to be that something.

From this standpoint, it is unreasonable to expect that the same children could imagine or pretend what it is like to be children who live in a developing nation and do not look like them. They cannot imagine what those children feel. If they cannot use their imagination to know what those children feel, they are much less likely to care about doing something to help those children. The ability to imagine how someone else feels increases the likelihood of wanting to help and to take action. This in turn, works to create a more equitable world.

While people do good works for the sake of good work, empathy helps increase the odds and sincerity of this process. Being able to imagine what it is like to starve, live in a war-torn country, or fear for one's safety leads to empathizing for people who suffer that plight. An increase in actually feeling what others feel increases willingness to act on their behalf, which may lead to increasingly working toward social justice.

The ability to empathize is gaining increased attention as we navigate a more connected, more transparent world. Empathy is being recognized as an essential skill in business, education, medicine—actually in all industries. Empathy helps one build connections, and these connections help one communicate, motivate, and encourage others more effectively.

The better one can understand others, the better one can understand oneself. Most importantly, empathy increases four skills necessary for decision-making and creative problem-solving: identity, cooperation, influence, and innovation. These skills are evident when we discuss blind spots, stakeholder groups, reflection, and developing creative solutions.

People empathize through one or more of three approaches. Empathy can be accomplished cognitively, somatically, or affectively. A person can try to think what someone else is thinking, have a physical response to what someone is doing, or feeling what someone is feeling. Cognitive empathy is the ability to think what someone else is thinking. Somatic empathy is when one has a physical response to what someone is doing or feeling. Affective empathy is the ability to feel what someone else is feeling.

Reviewing a situation through the eyes of someone familiar is the easiest way to understand these different empathetic responses. Picture a situation in which someone familiar (parent, child, significant other, good friend)—let's call this person Pat—is having a stressful week. What is the best approach to doing something nice for Pat?

In one scenario, it might be to take a few minutes and tidy up the space where Pat lives (presuming Pat would like this gesture). Now, using empathetic capabilities, what does Pat think when Pat realizes what was done (cognitive)? How does Pat feel (affective)? Does it bring a smile to think of Pat smiling (somatic)? Do shoulders relax in response to anticipating the relief Pat feels (also somatic)?

These are empathetic responses: the thoughts are cognitive empathy, the emotions are affective empathy, and the physical actions are somatic empathy. Stated more simply and practically, empathy can focus either on the thoughts, physical movements, or emotions of another person in order to be able to put oneself in the position of another.

The task at hand, when involved with decision-making and as a component of moral imagination, is to do this with respect to each of the stakeholders involved in the decision to be made. Consider the action of changing an organizational logo. How will each of the people this decision impacts respond to this change? As a leader, respond to this change in the persona of these people. If there are several large groups represented, imagine how a person or two from each group would respond.

The knowledge of how someone will respond to a decision, whether they are staff or community members, allows a decision maker to more effectively make and communicate about a decision. Decision makers can be more innovative once they imagine how those involved may choose to respond; empathy allows problem-solving capacity to expand by increasing scope and imagination.

There have been plans that seemed great, but when leaders engaged empathy and saw things through the eyes of others, the impact and potential response were negative enough to change or abort those plans. On a large scale, empathy is ethically necessary when contemplating how a policy may impact underserved groups, how curricular or social changes can have long-term developmental impact on students, or even how moving a school or creating a product can impact the environment.

Empathy allows prediction on a large scale, as well as on a small one. Consider what would happen if city planners empathetically worked through how zoning and housing issues would impact *all* stakeholders. Look back a century: How could the course of events in our national history look different if we had empathetically approached decisions that were made with the perspective of each stakeholder group that had been involved?

Approaching decision-making empathetically also allows for more effective communication. At the end of this process, when an effective solution has been created and a choice made, communication with all stakeholder groups, even those who may have advocated for a different outcome, is easier when time is taken to consider how each group may respond before a decision is shared. The decision can be shared, and the concerns and answers for each group involved can be addressed.

In pragmatic terms, the following is an example of how this can look on a daily level. A new director recently took over an organization.

The prior director had micromanaged all decisions. The new director smartly took the first week or so to watch what was going on and examine the responses of the people around him. One particular employee seemed pained when he came in and asked the director for permission and advice over small issues about running his buildings.

The director watched as the employee avoided eye contact, changed his physical stance, and lowered his shoulders when asking about situations the director knew he knew how to handle. The director could feel the mix of pain, anger, and slight humiliation this employee felt at having to run all decisions past someone else. The director used both cognitive and affective empathy to imagine what the employee was experiencing.

The director used his own empathy to imagine how the employee felt and imagined how he could put things in place that would help the employee move toward feelings of pride and confidence. The director told the employee he was responsible for the building. The employee and director set up periodic reviews versus daily ones.

Finally, the director communicated that he was always there if the employee had questions or wanted to run a solution past him, but beyond that, the employee was trusted to do his job. As a result, the employee is excelling, is dramatically more invested in his job, and is proactively creating new opportunities.

Chapter Eight

Consequences

One of the most important components of moral imagination is the time that is taken to consider the consequences of potential actions. This chapter will walk through how intended and unintended consequences should be considered in decision-making. Both the prediction of consequences and accessing empathy actively use imagination to envision something outside of one's immediate surroundings.

While many people may take time to consider the immediate, intended consequences of their actions, not many take time to consider the long-term consequences of their actions, and even fewer the possible but unintended consequences of their actions. As always, it is best to ask people directly how they will react to something, but in the absence of that option, imagination is key.

Consider how each stakeholder group may respond. In considering these possible responses, one is able not only to begin to discern what action may be the best course but also to troubleshoot and be prepared to explain why one course of action was chosen over another. Consideration of consequences provides the opportunity to solve for anticipated problems and imagine unanticipated ones. With potential problems identified, it is easier to create solutions ahead of time, make transitions go more smoothly, and keep stakeholders happier.

INTENDED, SHORT-TERM CONSEQUENCES

This is the easiest place to start. Considering the intended, short-term consequences is the most common thing that forward-thinking leaders do, if they do any thinking ahead or try to predict how things will play out at all. The first things to consider are the short-term, intended consequences of each potential action, for each stakeholder group.

What are the things that happen immediately if one pursues a particular course? What are the intended consequences for each stakeholder involved? If a person decides to move, what are the immediate consequences for friends, family, employers, service providers, neighbors, and self? One should start by considering what the picture looks like if everything goes as planned.

In this situation, the picture is that a person—let's call her Alice—has happily decided to move to pursue a brilliant opportunity. Intended consequences are that all things surrounding the move will go as planned. Alice is happy and excited. She has a great opportunity. She needs to find a place to live. She needs to convince her spouse to join her (it is presumed they like each other).

Alice will have to find a house that has enough room for her kids to stay when they come to visit. She has to be sure to have enough money to move and will create a timeline and checklist for completing all the necessary tasks to move. She may begin to decide what to do with the things she owns: move them, store them, sell them, or give them away?

Her friends will be excited for her. Her family will be supportive. Her employer, so thankful that Alice is direct and straightforward, will offer her the opportunity to work remotely versus move (remember: this is a best-case scenario) so that they can continue to work together. All of these things can be the intended or desired results of the decision to move.

The identification of intended consequences can also be used to help with goal setting. Having named her desired outcomes, Alice can choose to take steps to make sure these things happen. These are the immediate intended consequences. This example is a personal example, so there are not many stakeholder groups. It could be enlarged to include coworkers and those whom Alice serves in her job, but the group of people impacted is not as large as it would be if Alice were planning to shut down a school or move a business.

When a larger number of people are impacted, considering the short-term, intended consequences is a longer process. It is also interesting that one of the most common mistakes that happens in decision-making happens here. When leaders are going through this step, looking at the intended consequences of a course of action, problems arise if leaders have not looked at, or have actually overlooked, the impact on several stakeholder groups.

INTENDED, LONG-TERM CONSEQUENCES

After the possible short-term, intended consequences have been exhausted for each stakeholder group, the intended, long-term consequences need to be considered. Long-term goals are considered anything that takes over twelve months to accomplish, so consider long term consequences as things that may occur over a year after a decision is made.

The biggest long-term, intended consequence of Alice deciding to move is that she has actually moved. She has a new place to live and she loves it (again, these are the intended consequences; unintended consequences will be addressed in a bit). Alice has a job she likes. She is settled into a new place and has friends there.

The family and friends from where Alice previously lived are happy for her and even come to visit. Her adult children have moved to areas within an hour of where she is and/or are mobile, and Alice sees them as often as any of them want to see each other. Essentially, the long-term intended consequences of choosing to move are that Alice has moved and everything is wonderful.

Often people will consider short-term consequences in a pros/cons–type list when deciding to choose one thing over another. Often when forensic examination of past decisions occurs, it is the oversight of long-term consequences that has caused problems. While this happens with the intended consequences, it is often the failure to predict what may happen or consider something other than the outcome we want, which causes leaders to choose poorly.

UNINTENDED, SHORT-TERM CONSEQUENCES

It is relatively easy to predict the things that will happen when consideration is given to desired or intended consequences. It is harder to predict what may happen when one has to stretch to consider the unintended consequences of an action. It is easy for leaders to know what they want to have happen. It is harder to predict those things that are unintended. How does one determine what may occur? It requires employing empathy and imagination and being able to draw cause-and-effect lines from the decision that is made.

Consider this law of physics: energy is never lost nor gained; it is simply redistributed. If a decision is made to take something from one place or stop something in one place, the energy that has been going into that action/place is going to come out someplace else. The job of decision makers is to try to predict where this may happen. Consider each stakeholder group and, be honest, consider the worst possible sequence of events that can result from the decision.

As an example, one of the unintended consequences of the legalization of marijuana has been the short-term loss of income for low-level drug dealers. Until small-time dealers reorganize their business, they will see a loss following legalization. It's not something policy makers tend to consider, but it's an easy example of short-term, unintended consequences.

If we go back to the example above, regarding Alice's decision to move, when she decides to move there may be many unintended consequences as a result. In the short term, family and friends may be upset with the decision to move; they may feel abandoned or be hurt. They may think that Alice does not care about them or that they are not a priority for her.

Alice's current employer may fire her. She may not be able to find a job or a place to live. Her spouse may not want to go; he may decide that he cares about his job more than he cares about her and will resolve to stay put. There are so many things that may be unintentionally injured; Alice needs to stop and think about these things prior to making a decision.

These are the con points of the pros-and-cons list, and they need to be creative and all encompassing. This is also the creative strategy that involves planning for the worst possible circumstances. If one is building a zoo, one asks oneself how the animals may escape, and then one plans to prevent that from happening. One doesn't start by planning how it will look. Obviously, the animals escaping is another example of an unintended consequence, but using the strategy of planning for what one would not want to have happen provides another way to identify unintended consequences.

UNINTENDED, LONG-TERM CONSEQUENCES

Even more challenging than predicting short-term, unintended consequences is predicting the long-term, unintended consequences of a decision. What are the things that are not intended to happen but may happen as a result of this decision? Try to look ahead and think about what can occur. It is not easy. It is speculation, but it provides a leader with a basis for understanding what can go wrong and for planning in order to prevent it.

Use the same strategies as those used for predicting short-term, unintended consequences, and just look further out. Remember that "long term" is considered anything that occurs over a year after the decision is made. It is not often that people think that far ahead.

An example from a previous chapter, that of the governor who wanted to get computers for every school in his small, midwestern state, fits well here. The long-term, unintended consequences of spending money on computers and not providing infrastructure or professional development to support the teachers and schools that received the computers amounted to damage to the governor's professional credibility.

The governor's move to charge forward without consulting stake-holders (1) reinforced the teachers' impression that they were not heard by those who made the budgets and the laws, (2) wasted a lot of money, and (3) eliminated further support for computers because the schools had not used what they had been given.

Other examples of long-term, unintended consequences can be seen throughout history. We can see that the result of segregation was a system that was neither equal nor fair, that built resentments, and that created a dichotomy that continues to be hard to break. It seems obvious from our lens that if policy makers had considered how stakeholders would feel years down the road in response to events, a lot of pain could have been prevented.

Try to predict what may happen. Some consequences may be hard to see, but others, if one connects the dots, looks at the stakeholders, and reflects on past events, may seem easy.

Another example is that of federal student loan programs. Federal student loan programs were created to make college more accessible and provide the American dream to a greater cross section of the population, including those who did not have the advantage of the GI bill. While this has happened, to the extent that more people are attending college, what has also happened is that college costs have risen and loan amounts have risen with them, creating a system in which college is becoming prohibitively expensive to many.

It is not realistic for students to take out enough loans to cover the costs of college if doing so creates the untenable situation of student loan debt that is too high to manage upon graduation. The intended, long-term consequences of the federal student loan program were that more students would graduate from college. Unfortunately, the long-term, unintended consequences of the federal loan program are that many people took out loans that they could not afford to repay and the cost of college has increased dramatically.

Finally, there is the great example of the urban legend, the "Cobra effect" (Dunbar, 2012). As the story is told, many years ago, the British governor in India believed that there were too many cobras in Delhi and wanted to get rid of them. The governor had a bounty placed on cobras and offered to pay for each one that was killed and whose skin was brought into the administrative offices.

The governor expected this would solve the cobra problem. But the population in Delhi—at least some of it—responded by farming cobras. All of a sudden, the administration was getting too many cobra skins. The governor's office decided the scheme wasn't as smart as it initially appeared, and they rescinded the offer to pay for cobra skins.

Unfortunately, by then the cobra farmers had this little population of cobras. What happens when there is no market for a product? One gets rid of the product. The cobras were simply released by the farmers. Releasing the cobras worsened the cobra menace in Delhi. Had leaders predicted what could go wrong with offering a bounty on the cobras, this could have been avoided.

This is an oft-repeated example. This happens when humans become involved in species control. In the US Midwest, white-tailed deer have had a population boom and cause many automobile accidents. The rise in the population occurred due to the removal of natural predators that used to keep the population size in check.

Humans hunted the predators, and once the predators were removed, the deer population grew unchecked. The growth in population led to crowding in habitats and lack of food, which drove many deer into human communities. The deer often run into traffic, which causes the accidents. This is obviously an unintended, long-term consequence. While it is always hard to outguess what may happen, it is worth the time and effort to try to predict what the long-term consequences may be as the result of one choice over another.

Chapter Nine

Imaginative Solutions

While it has been said repeatedly that moral imagination is a cyclic process, the solutions are the goal. Now that all the homework has been done, the fun part comes. This is the time to use what has been learned to create the best possible outcome for those involved. Morally imagine what can make the most stakeholders happy and meet personal and/or organizational goals.

Once all the information that can be gathered has been gathered and the imagination is used to work empathetically and to predict possible consequences, it is time to consider what the possible solutions are. This chapter covers the importance of imaginative solutions. One of the consistent things about descriptions of moral imagination over time has been the role of moral imagination in creating morally sound decisions.

This step is the time to be creative. Take all of the information that has been gathered and, either independently or with stakeholders, create a picture of what the best outcome would be for all involved. This is the imaginative solution. It sounds easy, but it must be deliberate. How does this happen?

This is a place to bring in strategies to guide the thought process. Create templates; make predictions. This is also the time and the place to bring in others to help craft possible solutions; collaboration brings in more perspectives and often creates better ideas. There is substantial data from many industries that indicates that collaboration increases the efficacy of decision-making. In addition, creating imaginative solutions can be enjoyable and can involve a variety of possible ways to create options. The September/October 2018 issue of *Harvard Business Review*, along with other publications, sang the praises of design thinking (Liedtka, 2018) as a means to develop solutions to our ever changing, global community. If it is desirable to utilize design thinking at this point, please do so. It is fun, and it works. Just be sure to come up with more than one possible solution, Prototype more than one option; create choices. This works well in teams. Another option may be so-called creative problem-solving or whatever the organizational preference may be.

This is also a great place to bring in true, old-fashioned brainstorming. The information has been gathered, so now is the time to look at it, rearrange it, and create options. An idea for this brainstorming process, as follows, was gleaned from a Creative Education Foundation's Creative Problem-Solving workshop.

When brainstorming and coming up with ideas, rather than stop people when they begin to get ridiculous, encourage people to get ridiculous and unreasonable. It is on the other side of ridiculous that truly creative ideas emerge. A person must get past the social inhibitions that come with proposing ideas in front of colleagues before they are able to risk coming up with a real solution that approaches things in a new way (Parnes and Meadow, 1959).

Any of these things can be done alone, but as a leader, one might be well advised to employ one or more methods to increase creativity. Make an exhaustive list of what may happen, and just write down everything that comes to mind. Make a visual representation of what might work—that is, go beyond a list and do a mind map or a drawing.

In this step it is best to actually create a picture or scenario. Remember, this is creating a picture of what the best possible outcome will be, so what does it look like? Feel like? Smell like? Sound like? Employ the senses. How do the stakeholders respond? Imagine a conversation with them in which the plan for how to address the situation is being shared. How does it play out?

Please remember: it is a great idea to look for information and inspiration from other industries. If there is a problem in the education sector, is there something that has been done in health-care industry from which inspiration can be drawn? It is also ok to outright copy what has been done in another industry. Regardless of how possible solutions are created, try to create more than one so there are options from which to choose.

The background research has been done. Key players (stakeholders) have been identified, data in the forms of documents and interviews (antecedent events and conditions) have been gathered, and work has been done to actively predict how actions might play out for all of those involved (predicting consequences and empathy). All of the information has been compiled to make a solid decision.

This decision becomes imaginative when it creatively addresses the issues involved in a way that has never been used before. Creativity is developing or using components in a way that is novel and brings value. It is important to use solutions that have never been proposed to address problems that have never been seen.

The 2020 COVID-19 epidemic has been a great example of this. While there are many tragedies surrounding this situation, much innovation and creative problem-solving has occurred. Schools are the easiest example of how creative and imaginative solutions are created to address situations that have never been seen. Schools are adjusting scheduling and school hours to adapt to Centers for Disease Control and individual state requirements.

The results of creating imaginative solutions have been a variety of hybrid options. Some schools divided classes in half and are only having classes come half at a time, every other day, so the schools can be cleaned when classes are not in session. Other schools have gone entirely online. Other schools have required masks. Colleges are not taking breaks but are having students end semesters earlier so there is time for thorough cleaning at that point. Adaptations to the school year are as many now as there are types of schools.

Chapter Ten

Reflection

In order for this decision-making process to be considered moral imagination, it must include reflection. There is a need to critically review and evaluate what has happened in the past, carefully consider what may happen in the future, and determine how any possible solutions may play into both of these. Reflection is often the final step in the moral imagination process. Remember that moral imagination is not decision-making but a process for making decisions: it gets to the best options so a choice can be made.

Research indicates that reflection holds great value for leaders. Teachers, employers, and other leaders who take time to reflect on processes are more effective and demonstrate professional growth. In 2018, both *Forbes* and the *Harvard Business Review* shared articles stating the value of reflection in both motivation and great (yes, they used the word) leadership. Reflection has been named as one of the key competencies needed for effective leaders particularly as the workplace grows more complex and multicultural (Roberts, 2008).

Management guru Peter Senge (1990) placed the process of reflection at the center of organizational learning. Leaders must learn to review their actions, outcomes, and thought processes to learn from things that have gone well and make changes so that decision-making can occur much more smoothly in the future.

Relative to decision-making, reflecting on the information discovered, be it a blind spot that was previously left blind or a possible unintended consequence that makes a successful decision unlikely, ensures that the decision maker takes time and is considerate before moving forward with a decision. Taking time to reflect following each step is a good idea. It is also important to take time to reflect on the process as a whole. It is also critical before getting to the point of making a final choice.

Individuals may choose to reflect in a variety of ways. There are two things that need to happen regardless of the reflection method chosen: a leader must make time to reflect and a leader must be able to reflect free from distractions. One must make time to reflect: make an appointment or plan to reflect at a time when the brain will be relaxed, like while riding the bus or showering. Another option is to take time to journal.

Leaders may opt to find a "critical friend," someone with whom they can review their decisions and processes. In order for reflection to be effective, one must be free from outside distractions in order to actually think.

While reflecting on the moral imagination process, go through each component part:

Stakeholders
Conditions
Antecedent Events
Blind Spots
Consequences
Empathy
Creative Solutions and
Reflection

Has each part been considered? If the answer is no, ask, "Why not?" What would be the benefit of going back and completing the missing step? Go back and do the part that was missed.

Sometimes a person can get stuck on one part. When that happens, it is important to take a moment to reflect on what was learned and what is missing or not working. It is ok to reflect during and after each part; it is actually encouraged if there is time to do so. Consider some of the following questions.

When the blind spots are examined:

- What was learned?
- What changed about how the decision was being considered?

When stakeholders were identified:

- Was everyone considered?
- Is one group playing more prominently in the possible outcomes? Is that ok? Why or why not?
- Who is missing?

When considering antecedent events:

- Is there enough information to create a clear picture about what happened to bring the stakeholders and conditions to this point?
- Are the perspectives of the stakeholders collected relative to this history?

With regard to the conditions of the decision that needs to be made:

- Is there a clear picture of the setting?
- Are the nuances of this setting understood in a way that makes the decision different here and now than it may be some other place at some other time?

When the stakeholder groups are approached with empathy:

- Have all of the stakeholder groups been considered?
- Is honest consideration being given to how they may think, feel, or physically respond, or are the responses being assigned to them based on the responses that are desired?
- Are there solution options that can be eliminated because the response would make the option not worthwhile?

When one considers the possible consequences:

- Have all four levels of possible consequences—short- and long-term, intended and short- and long-term, unintended—been considered?
- Are there possible solutions or approaches that can be eliminated because the consequence would make it too complicated or not worthwhile?

- Are there approaches that rise to the top based on what has been predicted?

When one considers the possible solutions:

- Has the approach changed with all of the new thinking that has been done?
- Is there one answer that is clearly best for all?
- Are there one or two solutions that need to be examined more carefully?
- Is there more information that needs to be collected?

Once reflection is complete, if there is no need to go back and gather more information, consider how anyone else feels, or create more options, then the process is complete. The process of moral imagination has been utilized to come up with the best solutions. There are two things left to do: (1) choose and, then, (2) work to strategically plan the best way to implement the choice. Much of this should be laid out in one's intended and unintended consequences, but an actual plan for how to communicate and act on one's decision is what happens next. This is where one includes goals and objectives. Congratulations!

Chapter Eleven

Moral Imagination in Practice

Best-practice adult learning theory states that one of the best ways to engage adult learners is to provide relevant examples and attach information to prior learning. The following is provided with the hope that those who are actually working to solve problems in their daily lives may see that this as an effective way to help translate theory into active practice.

Decision-making with moral imagination can be used in two distinct ways. It can be used as a process to help create solutions, for individuals or organizations. It can also be used forensically to examine where an oversight occurred when things did not go as planned. Examples of moral imagination used for each purpose and from a variety of different places—industry, personal life, education, and not-for-profit realms—follow. All of these are real examples that have been edited to those involved anonymous.

Reflect

Identify
stakeholders

Engage creative
problem-solving

Outline
conditions

Engage empathy
for each
stakeholder
group

Examine
antecedent
events

Identify
consequences

Identify blind
spots

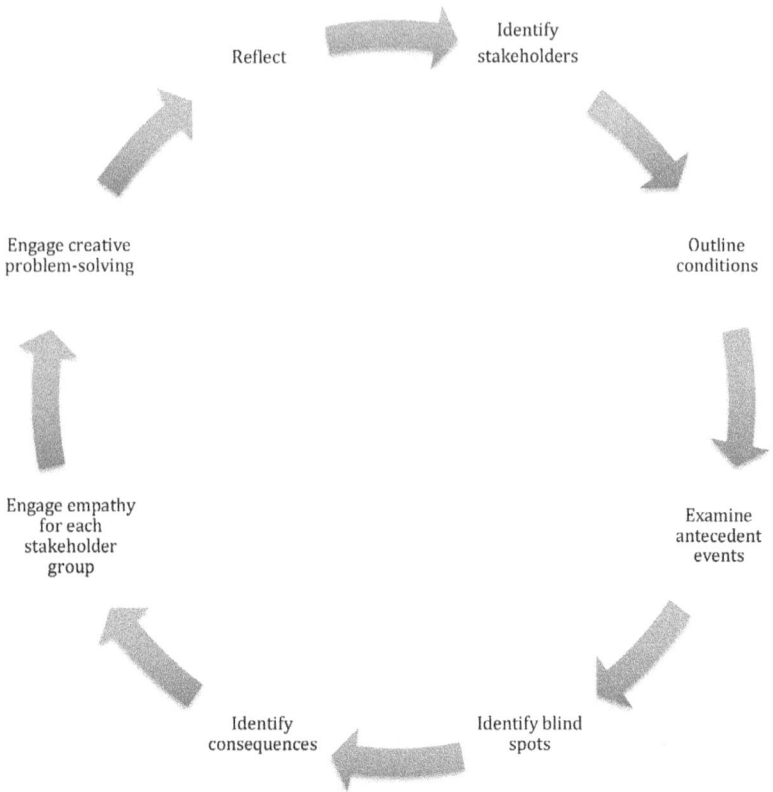

Figure 11.1. Moral Imagination Process
Sommervold Dissertation, 2010.

MORAL IMAGINATION AS A REVIEW PROCESS

As a way to help them understand the process and begin to be able to see the layers and perspectives that influence what we do on a daily basis, students are asked to bring forward decisions that did not turn out the way they had hoped and examine them through the lens of the moral imagination process. They are asked to review poor decisions from the past for an additional two reasons. First, review of past decisions demonstrates how the process can be used to help pinpoint what has been left out or overlooked in a decision. Second, the use of the moral imagination process to review past decisions helps decision makers understand the process of moral imagination as a credible way to move through the decision-making process and reach a desired outcome. When it is obvious that the process of moral imagination can help develop creative solutions that are more transparent and thoughtful, students are willing to bring it into their decision-making process.

The following are examples of how this process helped highlight the need to consider all aspects of moral imagination and made it easier to diagnose where decisions went wrong so leaders could reflect on these mistakes and correct for them in the future. This is what it looks like when the process of moral imagination is used forensically, to help people understand what went wrong where decisions did not play out as they would have hoped.

In each example, a summary will be provided, and then a list of the component parts of the moral imagination process will be outlined. The processes were copied verbatim from student work, and changes were not made. While the examples are good, it was deliberate choice that they not be examples of perfection; readers are encouraged to see where things worked and where they didn't, and to read between the lines to the unspoken connections.

EXAMPLE 1: THE TEACHER WHO WAS "GOOD ENOUGH"

A doctoral student who is an English instructional coach for a midsize rural district was charged with increasing the capacity of a teacher who was returning to the classroom after a hiatus. The teacher was struggling, and the coach was supposed to work with the teacher and get him back up to speed and providing solid instruction for his students.

Summary of Decision

One of the duties of an instructional coach is to work with teachers who have been placed on improvement plans. Through the winter and spring, an instructional coach worked with a middle school language arts teacher who was placed on an improvement plan to improve in his classroom instruction. Each week the coach and teacher met to focus on instructional strategies. During the time that the instructor was on the improvement plan, the coach observed the teacher in his classroom, taught with him, and taught model lessons in the classroom that the teacher observed.

One step toward helping the teacher improve was for him to teach a lesson while being videotaped and then for the coach to teach the exact same lesson and videotape it. The purpose was for the teacher to see the differences. The teacher was asked to watch the two lessons and be ready to reflect on what went well, what he was struggling with, and what the main differences were between the two lessons. When the time came for the teacher and coach to meet, the coach knew, through the view counter on YouTube, that the teacher had not prepared himself for the meeting. The coach met with the principal before meeting with the teacher and suggested that the videos needed to be watched with all three parties present: the teacher, the principal, and the coach; this would allow for open dialogue among all three.

When the time came for the weekly meeting, the teacher led with "I don't feel I need to meet with you anymore. I am a better teacher than this. I don't think I need to be on this plan." The coach agreed to share the teacher's feelings with the principal, told the teacher the principal would follow up, and ended the meeting.

Stakeholders

- *The Portal Public Schools superintendent and school board of the district.* The teacher was not being a proficient teacher while on an improvement plan and might not make enough improvements to have his contract renewed. If the teacher's contract was not renewed, the superintendent would have been involved, and the school board would have to approve the release of the teacher from the contract and the hiring of a new teacher.
- *The Portal Middle School principal.* He was responsible for evaluating the teacher and moved to placing the teacher on an improvement plan. He also suggested an instructional coach be written into the plan as a support to help the teacher improve.
- *The Portal Public Schools curriculum director.* It was her responsibility to provide teachers support with instruction and to make sure curriculum is being implemented with fidelity.
- *Portal Middle School counselors.* They were dealing with students experiencing frustrations as a result of this class: they needed to

make schedule changes for students who were failing the struggling teacher's language arts classes; they also had to counsel students who did not want to take more language arts classes or that language arts class in particular.

- *Portal Middle School students in the struggling teacher's language arts classroom.* They were frustrated with not understanding the material that was being taught due to poor instruction.
- *Fellow Portal Middle School language arts teachers.* In the future, they would get the struggling language arts teacher's students in their classes. These students will come to their classes without the background knowledge needed to be successful.
- *Portal Middle School students not in the struggling teacher's classroom.* They would have to help struggling students answer language arts questions.
- *After-school tutoring teachers.* Their student numbers would go up due to the questions and language arts help the students needed.
- *Parents.* They would be dealing with frustrated children and might not be in a position to help their children understand the material.
- The struggling language arts teacher. He was the one on an improvement plan and, as a result of the lack of improvement, could lose his job.
- *The district instructional specialist.* It was her job to coach the teacher to improve his craft and become proficient.

Antecedent Events

- The previous language arts teacher had resigned late in the year, which meant the pool of quality applicants was smaller than it would have been closer to January (the implication being that the language arts teacher was maybe not the best candidate).
- A current language arts teacher at the middle school was friends with the struggling teacher and encouraged him to apply for the language arts job at the middle school.
- The struggling language arts teacher had been out of the K–12 classroom for a long time, and his skills were lacking and not up to date.
- The district pushes students to challenge themselves, which translates to harder classes. So students who might potentially be borderline candidates for lower-level English classes were now pushed to take

more difficult courses, which are the classes the struggling teacher taught.

Conditions

- This took place at Portal Public Middle School, a middle-class school in a midsize community in the Midwest in 2013, with 6th–8th grade students in the language arts I classroom.
- The principal had performed evaluations of the teacher, which led to many conversations with the teacher about his struggles.
- Many parents had called the counseling office and the principal to discuss their child not understanding the material that was being presented in the class. They said the teacher was not providing help.
- Students were going to the counselors to ask what help was available for them to understand the content or to ask to move to a different teacher or class.
- Fellow teachers were coming to the principal's office to express concerns about the teacher's mental health and his instruction in the classroom, based upon what they were hearing from the students.
- Counselors met with the principal to discuss the current situation with the students coming in and asking for help and not understanding the content. The counselors also shared with the principal that this involved by far more students than would come in during a typical year.
- The instructional coach was called into a meeting with the teacher and the principal, and together they developed a plan of what it would look like for the teacher to get off the improvement plan. During the meeting, the struggling teacher seemed very receptive to changing his instruction and meeting with the instructional coach.
- The instructional coach and teacher started meeting once a week, every week, for 10 weeks. It was toward the end of the 10 weeks when the incident happened.

Empathy

- The superintendent and school board want the district to have the highest-quality teachers and, even though a nonrenewal of contract can be hard and can drag out with a hearing—if it comes to that—ultimately, they still want the best instruction for their students.

- The middle school principal's job is to evaluate teachers and make sure the teachers are meeting the needs of the students in the classroom. Also, the principal must respond to the concerns of the parents and students not understanding the material due to poor teaching and to reteaching not taking place in the classroom.
- The curriculum director supports new teachers by sending them to professional development days before the school year starts to have them gain an understanding of instructional strategies that can be used in the classroom. At the time, the district was in transition from its current model to a possible new model of instruction, and the professional development did not align to its new model. This meant new teachers needed more support than was originally planned.
- The Portal Middle School counselors were feeling frustrated because they wanted the students to succeed. When students struggle, they want to find every opportunity to help the students find success. When the core issue is lack of good instruction, this is not an area the counselors can directly fix or improve in their current roles.
- The Portal Middle School students were feeling very frustrated and wanted to understand the content or just get out of the class. No student wants to fail, and if there is a chance of failing, it can be scary for the student and cause a flight response.
- Fellow middle school language arts teachers were frustrated because they were hearing there was not good instruction taking place in the classroom. The teachers knew that they would then be responsible for filling in the gaps of the poorly taught students who would arrive in their classrooms, on top of teaching their own class material.
- Portal Middle School students who were not in the language arts class of the struggling teacher were feeling pressure from the students who were in the class to help them understand the material. This, in turn, took time away from the students working on their own homework or doing something else they enjoyed.
- Parents ultimately wanted their child to succeed, and when they saw their child struggle, they wanted to provide help in whatever way they could. If they were not able to help by themselves, parents might hire a tutor if they had the money; otherwise, they turned to calling and talking to the principal about why the teacher was not appropriately helping their child understand the material.

- The struggling language arts teacher was dealing with a lot outside of school—money was tight, and his spouse was an alcoholic—on top of being put on an improvement plan because he was not meeting minimum standards in the classroom. He definitely had many concerns and issues, might not always have been focused on the tasks in the classroom, and was not always prepared for the lessons of the day.

Blind Spots (in the Words of the Person Who Wrote Them)

"I like to always assume the best in people; therefore, I always start by giving them the benefit of the doubt about their ability. After meeting with the struggling teacher, I learned more about his deficits and lack of skill. He had no ability to plan, and it led to no idea of where he was going and what was coming next or what had been covered. Students' lack of understanding was a result of there being no consistent flow or structure in the classroom.

"After observing the teacher, I realized he was not providing enough examples for the students to practice with and ask questions about before beginning their homework. There was also little to no time during or at the end of the class period for students to get started on their homework and be able to ask questions if they had questions.

"The teacher was not checking students' homework or providing the students correct answers to their homework, so students were not sure if they understood the material or not until it came time for the test and they flunked. All of these were blind spots going into the meetings with him and that were discovered through observations.

"My blind spots were literal, in that I did not understand the extent of the situation, until I saw it firsthand. As they were tied to my core values, my blind spots were that everyone wanted to and always did work as hard as they were able, that classroom teachers had been well trained and understood what needed to happen in order for students to learn, and that each person wanted to be the best at what s/he was doing and that people sought feedback to do a better job."

Consequences (of Putting an Unprepared Teacher into the Classroom)

Short-term, intended: students had a language arts teacher for the year.
Short-term, unintended:

- students struggled to understand material in the classroom and became frustrated with the class and the teacher.
- students failed the class due to not understanding the material and then had to retake the class before being able to move on to another language arts class.
- students acted out or gave up in the classroom because of a lack of understanding and therefore became a behavior problem.

Long-term, intended: obviously, the long-term, intended consequences are that the teacher utilize the resources at hand and improve to the point of being able to continue the following year.
Long-term, unintended:

- students may struggle in future language arts classes due a lack of the basic understanding of the concepts that were to be mastered in this teacher's classroom.
- students may fall behind in the language arts classes they need in order to graduate or may not graduate on time.
- students may struggle later on the ACT/SATs in the language arts section and may not get a high enough score to get into the college of their choice.
- parents have to pay for a tutor or send their child to tutoring provided through the middle school and will miss family time in the evening.
- the teacher may end up getting released from his current contract due to not meeting minimum requirements set forth by the district.
- other teachers may become frustrated due to the lack of basic knowledge of language arts concepts of students coming from the struggling teacher's class and due to having to reteach concepts, thereby getting behind in their own curriculum.
- Students' state test scores will lower, and the school will not meet AYP (adequate yearly progress).
- the school could end up having a lower graduation rate due to students failing the language arts class.

Creative Solutions (Including Words of the Person Who Wrote Them)

- To reach out to various teacher colleges to do more recruiting of teachers instead of just posting the job and accepting the applicants that were received. This would have allowed for a different applicant pool to pick from and interview.
- To have the teacher turn in weekly lesson plans from the beginning. This would have allowed for the principal to catch the teacher's lack of planning ability right from the start. The solution could have been to make all new teachers turn in weekly lesson plans until they proved to be proficient planners in the classroom.
- To implement a true mentoring program in the district in order to provide all new teachers the support and guidance they need from fellow teachers. "That is now part of my job but should have been in place last year in order to help all new teachers."
- To do a nonrenewal of contract for the teacher ("there was enough evidence") and "be able to get a better teacher earlier in the hiring time frame instead of June. The fact that the teacher continues to be in the district and struggle is only hurting our students."

Reflection (in the Instructional Coach's Words)

"Now looking back at my choice of stating what would happen and ending the meeting, I would not choose that same approach now. I have reflected a great deal about different ways I could have handled the situation. Knowing what I know now, about how awkward the relationship was between the teacher and me, I should have tried to flip the conversation around and get down to the root problems, versus ending abruptly.

"I would have taken more time to talk with him about why he was on the plan, why we were wanting to view the lesson together with him, and other issues that were impacting him in the classroom, as there were many personal issues he was also having. I needed to coach him through the issues more than I did and hold him accountable for his action of not watching the videos. In the end I needed to be an advocate for all the students struggling in his class.

"I should have helped guide him through the process of improving better than what I did. The teacher is currently still teaching at the middle school, and the relationship between the two of us is now awkward, since there has been no follow-up between us, other than an apology from him to me about his reaction."

Reflecting on the process and using it as a diagnostic tool allowed the instructional coach to see how she could have approached the situation differently, and during a visit with her, she stated that the process helped her better understand the bias she brought to the teachers she coached and that her blind spots were based on her background.

In evaluating this process, what else went wrong? In which step did it occur?

EXAMPLE 2: WHERE TO DRAW THE LINE

This example details the experience of a school district that reconfigured boundaries.

Stakeholders

- Students and families on the west side and the east side of the Blacktail School District
- Administrators
- Community at large
- Services dependent upon district guidelines

Antecedent Events

The Blacktail Public Schools District conducted a study of attendance projections for the next ten years. This study forecasted continued growth in the western part of the district while enrollments would decline in the eastern part of the district. Blacktail West High School's enrollment was growing by hundreds of students a year, while Blacktail East's enrollment was steadily declining.

Prior to this, the district had told people that they would not have to move. The district did not anticipate the growth or the growth pattern that it began to see. This is a contemporary issue and was resolved within the last ten years in a midwestern state.

Conditions

Overall enrollment in the district was slowing down to roughly 1 percent increase a year. The northern part of the district was holding steady because of open-enrollment students from the Northland Public Schools District as well as other districts. The western part of the district was growing rapidly because of new construction and the sale of existing homes.

The eastern part of the district was growing older, with fewer school-age children and low turnover of housing leading to declining enrollment. The boundaries were redrawn, but students all the way down to fourth grade in some instances were given grandfathering privileges to attend their currently assigned school.

The social conditions were very rigid. Families that were assigned to Blacktail West High School did not want to move schools. Some of the parents who came to the board meeting to speak out against the boundary change had students that were still in elementary school. This illustrates some of the passion and emotion surrounding this topic. The extended grandfathering also created some emotion, because not all neighborhoods were given the option to grandfather.

Empathy

Redrawing attendance boundaries is one of the most controversial and emotional tasks a district will face. Neighborhoods and families become attached to their assigned school, and most students and parents do not want to go to a different school. The students and parents affected by the new attendance boundary lines will be emotional.

- Leaders face moving families and being accused of unfairly drawing the boundary one way or another.
- Parents face the possibility of moving their kids or dealing with increased travel time getting kids to school. They may be sad if they have to split siblings or move students away from schools to which they have an emotional attachment.
- Students face uncertainty, and while a few may welcome a switch, most are apprehensive about moving.
- Neighbors without school-age kids may not want more kids around or may be excited about the move.

- Local officials will not be able to please everyone and need to be prepared to address this with constituents.
- Bus drivers may have new routes.
- Street services (snow removal, repair, etc.) may have changing roles or priorities.
- Home prices may reflect district line changes, and in either direction; it could decrease the value of some homes and increase the value of others.

Blind Spots

Blacktail West High School is overcrowded, and that can create a blind spot to the wants and needs of some families in the district because there was a need to force more students to attend Blacktail East, where there is building capacity.

Some of the families may have very legitimate academic needs or concerns as to why they should stay at Blacktail West. Some needs may have been social and emotional as to why they wanted to stay at Blacktail West. Either way these are, again, potential blind spots.

Personal blind spots [per a school district representative] include believing that students have to move, that the administration is doing the best it can, that people understand why district lines have to move, and that students and families are adaptable.

Consequences

A community divided.

- Short-term, intended consequences: Boundaries are redrawn and as many people are happy as humanly possible. Staff, students, parents, and community adjust well, and there is room for everyone to do what they need to do.
- Short-term, unintended consequences: A district representative said, "Boundary revisions can sometime bring out the worst in people. Community members showed their ugly sides. Statements like, 'I do not want my son/daughter to have to go to the poor school,' become disheartening and cause hurt feelings among the community. We had these comments and worse made in public session at our board meetings. It was ugly."

- Long-term, intended consequences: The redrawing, while not as smooth as hoped, will provide students, families, and community members with the resources they need to be successful. Everyone finds a place in the new order of things.
- Long-term, unintended consequences: Permanent rifts and lack of trust occur within the community. Rather than send their students to a school that they do not want, parents are open-enrolling their students back into the old school, another district, or a private school. Families from the "poor" school are not treated well. The students are in a new place and feel resented. Families become less involved in school because they do not feel welcome.

Reflection

Says the district rep, "Redrawing the boundary lines was essential to the future of our district. We needed to draw more students back to the east to get more efficient use of our buildings and to prevent overcrowding. Because of the angry outcry from some parents, we compromised too much on the grandfathering clause that will force us to deal with boundary issues related to Blacktail West for the next eight years."

Creative Solutions

Again, quoting the district representative:

"The biggest common issue every year is families who move out of the Blacktail West attendance area and they want their students to stay enrolled at Blacktail West. Our answer to this has been 'no,' unless the parents can provide a medical (social/emotional) rationale as to why the student should be able to stay at Blacktail West. Once word got out on this, we had many families that were producing notes from psychologists and psychiatrists as to why it was medically necessary for the well-being of the student to stay at Blacktail West.

"This year we will be more allowing of students who move out of the Blacktail West attendance area, but stay within the District of Blacktail to continue their enrollment at Blacktail West. If they still live within district boundaries and had already attended Blacktail West, we will allow them to stay in most circumstances. For those that move out of the district, we will not allow them to remain enrolled at Blacktail West, because it is a closed school. We will need to propose some changes to policy in order for these changes to take place. The changes will need approval from the school board."

The person quoted could identify the negative impact of the choice to grandfather students in and saw that because the administration was concerned with making everyone as happy as possible, the district would have to go through the same process in about eight years. If they look at who all the stakeholders are and empathetically identify what issues may arise, this process may go more smoothly next time.

This is a great example of how a recently past decision becomes an antecedent event. Now community members will hold onto the fact that they "just had" to redraw district lines. This redrawing so soon will color how many people feel about moving forward. As the reader, what else can you see that could have been done differently?

The previous examples demonstrated how the moral imagination process could be used as a diagnostic tool. The following is an example of how to use the process to make a decision.

AN EXAMPLE OF MORAL IMAGINATION AS A DECISION-MAKING PROCESS

A director at Cedarwoods, university in the Midwest, is working with the dean and weighing the professional decision to open a new concentration for the doctorate of education program. The doctoral program is relatively new but has been up and running for five years now. As it emerges, it is becoming clear that not everyone is interested in a doctorate in education with an emphasis in educational leadership.

The team is working on the idea of opening a concentration in "community and cultural relationships." This example will be used to work through a current issue with the process of making a decision with moral imagination.

As one becomes more familiar with the moral imagination process, it becomes obvious that it is not always used linearly. This is exactly how the process is used while a group is going through the decision-making process.

Blind Spots

It is good to examine blind spots early in the process and again later. The director's blind spots regarding starting programs are:

- He is arrogant about starting programs, believing he can build anything within the context of Cedarwoods and that it will be good.
- He forgets that many people do not like change.
- He forgets that the people who helped set the stage for the EdD program may not want this; it may not be part of the initial vision.
- He likes to start things.
- He thinks everything in the current program can be handled and sustained while work is done on the new program.
- He believes he has time to do it.
- He tends to just move forward, sometimes without regard to whether all the stakeholders are ready.
- He has not asked everyone; he believes that once everyone can address their feelings about the program and ask questions, everyone will be ok with it.

It is hard to actually write something down and not actively consider it at the same time. The process of reflecting on how a leader has behaved in past situations and how the leader tends to behave becomes obvious when one is forced to articulate blind spots and put them to paper. As the blind spots in this situation are reviewed, it is really apparent that the director may want this more than others, because he likes to bowl ahead. The director needs to approach people cautiously and gently and not run them over.

Stakeholders

- Current students
- Future students
- Alums of the EdD program
- Cedarwoods alums
- Cedarwoods administration
- Dean
- Provost
- Current graduate education professors

- Current graduate education program directors
- Instructors
- Cedarwoods St. Paul staff
- Cedarwoods Minneapolis staff
- Cedarwoods students
- Cedarwoods Winona staff
- Director
- Director's family
- Education liaison

Conditions

Among the current conditions surrounding this decision are:

- Spring 2021
- Academic year 2020–2021
- Midwestern state
- Small college turned university, with a traditional campus in a small rural town and three larger campuses—two in metro areas and one in a small, remote, city farther west
- Tight market for traditional four-year colleges
- Graduate education team experiencing turnover
- Graduate program that is financially supporting a small traditional campus
- Interim dean

Antecedent Events

This can get complicated. In this case, the history and workings of the College of Education come in as important pieces of what has led to this moment. Now on "Community 7," the Cedarwoods education specialist program began seven years ago—three years before the first doctoral cohort. When the education specialist (EdS) program began, the (then) dean and the director envisioned a program that fed smoothly into a doctoral program. They pictured an EdD program with an emphasis on educational leadership.

Prior to the EdS program, Cedarwoods had built a successful education leadership program: a master's of education degree that qualified participants for a principal's endorsement in the state. Over thirty cadres had completed the MEdL program. This large base was the main impetus for beginning the EdS program. One fed into the other.

Cedarwoods did things better, and the students who went through Cedarwoods wanted to have an EdS program that focused on dispositions and building servant leadership rather than simply checking off the requirements necessary to get the degree.

Cedarwoods education programs have a solid history of creating thoughtful leaders. Legend has it that when the current director of the EdS program was trying to decide between taking the job with Cedarwoods or taking a job with a competitor, he went to several schools in the area and asked whose program they would choose if they had to hire a teacher or principal sight unseen, just based on where the hire had gone to school.

All of them said Cedarwoods was the best, so he took the job with Cedarwoods. Cedarwoods also guarantees its results: if one hires an administrator from Cedarwoods and the hire poses a problem, the program director will come and help out for as long as is necessary.

As a result of these factors, Cedarwood's doctorate of education with an emphasis in educational leadership was born. The dan, the director of the EdS program, and a few professors from the undergraduate program pulled the framework of the courses together. The current director was hired to create the program from the existing framework.

Course titles and credit hours were determined, but the rest of the programming—the course instructors, books, content, and sequence—was organized by the current director. Students who had successfully completed the EdS degree at Cedarwoods were automatically admitted into the doctoral program; the EdS courses transferred in and fulfilled twenty-seven of the fifty-seven credits required for the program. These students were all administrators who had an interest in leadership.

When it came time to decide the program prerequisites, a master's degree with a minimum grade point average of 3.0 and a writing sample were the academic requirements. Students from programs outside of education leadership began to apply to the doctoral program. Most significantly, students from the master of education in curriculum and instruction (C & I) began to apply, as did students from master's in counseling and master's in management programs.

It became clear that the doctoral program had a broader appeal than had initially been considered. Not all students applying were interested in a doctorate with a focus in educational leadership. Because they want a doctorate from Cedarwoods, many have pursued the EdD with educational leadership although their interests were different.

When all of these programs began, there was a campus in Winona, one in St. Paul, and one in Duluth. Since the EdD began, a Minneapolis campus has been created. Fifty percent of the students in the doctorate program are from the Minneapolis area, although all of the graduate education courses are taught in St. Paul.

When the Minneapolis campus opened, one of the two directors of the MEdL program moved to Minneapolis and opened a permanent cadre presence there. While other graduate education classes are periodically offered on that campus, no other program has established a program base there.

In May 2019 the woman who had been dean for over twenty years retired. The following April, the education department was turned into a College of Education. In January, two years prior, the school had transitioned from a college to a university so it could bring in international students and more fully support a doctoral program.

The leadership changed, but with the exception of the assistant to the dean, the dean and the provost, the staff within the graduate education program has stayed the same. While the provost was new to Cedarwoods last year, the interim dean is from Cedarwoods and has taught as a professor in the undergraduate program and in the doctoral program.

Last year the director, educational liaison, and professor from Cedarwoods who are associated with the doctoral program all travelled to Argentina to present at a conference and collaborate with faculty at an Argentinian university. This travel prompted discussions about what international courses within the graduate education program would look like.

Simultaneously, discussions from the doctoral advisory council and within the graduate education staff have circled around the idea of offering classes with urban and rural focuses. The new programming will have concentrations in global and urban and rural community and cultural organizations. Finally, the subject of COVID came up. As this program is considered, what are the implications of starting a new program at a time when the future of higher education is uncertain?

Empathy

As the idea of starting a new program is contemplated, it is important to empathetically consider what stakeholders may think and how they may feel.

Table 11.1. Comparison of Moral Imagination and Best Practice Decision-Making.

Stakeholder(s)	Empathetic Response to Opening a New Program
Current students	May be bitter because this wasn't offered when they started. Some may ask if they are able to transfer because they either do not want a focus in educational leadership or they may not want to travel to St. Paul for classes. Many students may not care.
Future students	Will be happy to have the option of dual locations and an alternate emphasis. May have limited options if class size gets too small.
Alums of EdD program	Happy to have the program expand. Concerned about it growing too fast and/or the program maintaining its good reputation.
Cedarwoods Alums	Same as EdD alums.
Cedarwoods Admin	Depends: Some will be happy, but there is some latent competition between the programs, so admin from other programs may hope that the attention and permission to grow will be directed at their program. All will have to be sold on the program and know the positive aspects of it.
Dean	Excited to start something new. Happy to grow programs and provide options that are not leadership focused. Concerned about the program quality and the relationships within the graduate education programs; wants to ensure that adding another program adds markets but does not pull from the existing programs. Curious about what will happen to this new programming if a new dean is chosen a year after the program starts.
Provost	Excited to start something new. Happy to grow programs and provide options that are not leadership focused. Concerned about the program quality and the relationships within the graduate education programs; wants to ensure that adding another program adds markets but does not pull from the existing programs.

Stakeholder(s)	Empathetic Response to Opening a New Program
Current graduate education professors	Will welcome the possibilities of new programming and creating new classes. Most professors, other than being concerned for whether they will be asked to teach, will not care at all.
Current graduate education program directors	The director of the MEd in school counseling is excited about it, as is the director of the MEd in C & I. The directors from the leadership programs (MEdL and EdS) are rightly concerned about whether it will draw students away from the EdL classes, about who will create and teach the new courses, and about how they will be evaluated.
Cedarwoods St. Paul staff	Generally neutral, with the exception of being concerned about having to take on additional responsibilities that are based in Minneapolis.
Cedarwoods Minneapolis staff	The inverse of the St. Paul staff: excited and happy to have the space used but concerned about how the work and the responsibilities will play out for them.
Cedarwoods Omaha students	Happy to have options but, if concerned at all, concerned about sharing resources and space.
Cedarwoods Winona staff	May be happy, because new exposure for Cedarwoods often brings new students, which brings job security. They may also have the same apprehensions as the Cedarwoods St. Paul staff. Systems for newly expanded programming are just getting ironed out between Winona and St. Paul, and another location adds another set of logistics.
Director	Excited about starting a new program but has the same concerns as the other graduate education professors. Concerned about drawing students and instructors for a new program but believes that if orchestrating the new emphasis well is figured out, it will be very beneficial and desirable for many students.
Director's family	Always excited for the director to take on new challenges but also concerned that the director will take on more than is manageable. Concerned that the director will dive into something too deeply that requires more time than is available.
Educational liaison	The education liaison for the EdD program is excited. Wants to create programming that is forward thinking and promotes social justice; to that end, is excited about a program that will address the issues facing global, rural, and urban schools. But also concerned about how this will affect status and duties.

Possible Consequences

The brain wants to examine the empathetic response in great detail; maybe it is human nature to want to examine how others feel and respond. It works best if at this point, one gets the possible consequences sorted out, too, and then reflects on the responses and consequences as a whole. When utilizing this process, all individuals and organizations should do what works for them; that may mean a short period of reflection at the end of each step or it may mean completing several steps prior to reflecting. Try it both ways; do what works best.

Short-term, intended consequences. The immediate intended consequences of creating an additional program in at one of the other Cedarwoods locations are to increase options for students pursuing a doctorate and to increase enrollment. The program addition will also increase the visibility of the school and increase enrollment in other Cedarwoods schools. It will not be additional work for staff or professors at any of the locations.

The program director, educational liaison, professors, and dean will have the satisfaction of creating a program that addresses a need and works toward providing equitable educational experiences in global, urban, and rural environments and that fulfills the desire to create something new. Alumni and current and future students will be pleased to be part of a tradition of innovation and to have more options to address unmet needs in the state.

Long-term, intended consequences. The long-term, intended consequences of adding an additional program align with, and are largely continuations of, the short-term, intended consequences of this situation. Long term, the intended consequences are that the program will be successful and self-promoting and that the students will complete their research and dissertations at high levels and go on to teach and do research that further benefits community and cultural relationships.

The program will make money. The staff and faculty will all be happy with the additional program in a new location, and it will not be an extra strain on anyone. The dean will be happy to have chosen to support this program and will no longer be interim. The program director will be happy to have chosen to move forward and to have presented with the education liaison and collaborated in rural, urban, and global settings. Cedarwoods—past, present, and future—will be happy with the program's success and the way it reflects on the administration and culture of the institution.

Short-term, unintended consequences. Unintended consequences are largely harder to envision. This arena is the place where the imagination is truly key. How does one predict what may not go as planned? As hard as it is, the easiest way to predict the unintended consequences is to envision what the situation looks like if everything goes wrong. In the Cedarwoods example, the short-term unintended consequences can head in one of two directions: one is that the program does not begin—that something happens, and the decision is made to not start the program.

The second unintended consequence is that the program begins but it starts slowly and limps along. There are just enough students to start the program but too few to have teams of instructors or warrant new faculty; staff and faculty fears are relevant, and the current teams wind up doing extra work for a program that barely gets going. Several instructors are so disenchanted with the program that they leave to teach in other programs and do not recommend that students attend the Cedarwoods program.

Long-term, unintended consequences. The long-term, unintended consequences of starting the Cedarwoods doctorate of education with an emphasis in community and cultural relations would be that it ends or goes poorly. The worst unintended consequence would be that it goes so poorly that students are hurt by bad information or bad instruction and spend money but do not finish.

Reflection

The reflective piece of all of this is always very interesting. It was not until it was typed out that the need to handle this situation delicately became so very obvious. The only unintended consequences that could negatively impact anyone have to do with lack of planning, poor programming, or poor instruction, and all of these things are preventable. Again, as the nature of the director is to jump into things, this is a good reminder that beginning a new program has to be handled with care.

Reflection on the empathetic responses and approaches to the various stakeholders also supports the idea of moving deliberately but slowly with the other program directors and the staffs at the various campuses. The program and processes need to be carefully outlined so there is not confusion and so program directors and the dean can see that the work is equitably distributed. Communication will be key, so each stakeholder knows what is happening and how each will benefit by supporting a new program.

Finally, as the conditions and possible consequences indicate, there is a danger of drawing students from other programs and ostracizing the other program directors. There is also a need to make sure the programming and content is strong. Reflection includes the director's responses to previous situations like this; the beginning of the current doctoral program five years ago went well but could have gone more smoothly if more time had been devoted to the administrative details.

Creative Solutions

This is the place for imagination. There are many ways to come up with solutions: brainstorming or simply finding answers within the imagination. With the information that has been uncovered in the steps leading up to this point, the choices that can be made are varied. The obvious choice that needs to be made is whether or not to start a new program.

The reflection upon the stakeholders, antecedent events, possible consequences, and even the blind spots of the decision maker does not indicate that there are any dire consequences for choosing to begin a new program. Past the decision to begin the program, reflection indicates that there are communication and administrative issues that need to be handled carefully and need to be addressed in the strategic planning and goal setting associated with the decision.

And the process is complete. Complete-ish. When a process involves reflection, it takes a cyclic rather than linear progression. Once a decision is made, the process and resulting conclusion can be reflected upon. Reflection can pinpoint places the process could have gone more smoothly and how things can be done differently next time.

This is now the place where leaders bring in strategic planning and begin to set tangible goals and objectives. Information that was gathered during the process can help guide strategic planning. The places from the moral imagination process that caused extra consideration or seemed problematic may require careful handling; plans should be developed to address these issues.

As an example, stakeholders who may be defensive or territorial about a new program need to be brought into the planning and creation to secure buy-in and address any questions or concerns they may have. Scheduling issues that caused staff to avoid the idea of a new program can be addressed early on, so calendars work smoothly from the beginning.

Leaders can address larger moral issues directly and not be afraid of being questioned. It is reassuring to know that, as a leader, one has examined an issue completely and, while one may not agree with everyone involved, one can be transparent about how a decision was reached because the fact is that every vantage point has been considered.

Chapter Twelve

Moral Imagination for Organizational Decision-Making

The components of moral imagination can be used in organizational decision-making the same way as when they are used by individuals. This chapter examines the nuances of moving the process from the individual to the organizational level. There are some specific adaptations that occur when a group is completing this process. Earlier, the components of moral imagination were organized in to three distinct categories. These categories become important when approaching this

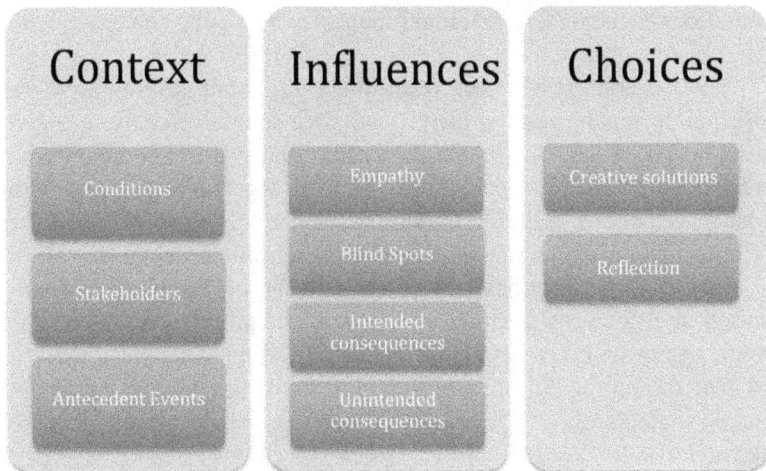

Context	Influences	Choices
Conditions	Empathy	Creative solutions
Stakeholders	Blind Spots	Reflection
	Intended consequences	
Antecedent Events	Unintended consequences	

Figure 12.1.   Three Components of Moral Imagination
Sommervold Dissertation, 2010.

process as an organization because they provide delineation for which parts are done individually and which parts are done as a group. The language of context, influences, and choices will help direct participants through the process.

Once it has been decided that a board or committee will go through the moral imagination process as a group, time is set aside for the group to meet. If this process is being done in one sitting, plan on at least a half day. A facilitator is appointed to help walk the group through this process.

Prior to gathering, each participant (including the facilitator) has the homework of compiling an independent picture of the context of the decision. Who is involved? What has happened? What is our setting? The first thing a facilitator will do is bring everyone together and create a combined list of the context: the conditions, stakeholders, and antecedent events. While the facilitator will not share the list, it is necessary for this person to create it in order to prompt others to think more inclusively and completely about a situation if, collectively, the group is forgetting or deliberately leaving out pieces of information.

Compiling the context of the decision first allows a concrete step to be completed, sets a tone of having the committee work together, and allows everyone in the group to get a feel for the varying perspectives of the group members. One of the good things about using moral imagination with groups is that going through process of identifying conditions, stakeholders, and blind spots may help build consensus with the decision-making team.

Once the context has been determined, the group will either work together or in subgroups to identify possible solutions for the question at hand. The group as a whole will reflect and work to come up with creative solutions. First, subgroups will work together to come up with what they believe is the best solution and then, in the wake of those solutions, they will examine the influences to rolling out a plan.

Once all subgroups have come up with the best choice, they will present their choices and their rationale to the group as a whole. The whole group will then decide on the best decision. This piece looks a lot like the prototyping phase of design thinking and could bring in brainstorming from creative problem-solving to help get the creative juices flowing.

THE PROCESS OF MORAL IMAGINATION FOR STRATEGIC PLANNING

Once the best possible solution has been chosen, any strategic-planning process can be brought in to create a plan and set goals and objectives toward the ideal situation. As a process that facilitates strategic-planning meetings for area organizations, moral imagination has been a useful tool to bring board members together.

The points of moral imagination work when choosing the direction an organization should travel. As has been demonstrated, determining the blind spots of an organization can help create a plan to compensate for the areas that have been lacking. An organization in a traditionally homogenous community may be missing opportunities to bring in new community members. The oversight of including new people may simply be the result of an organization not recognizing that its stakeholder group has grown.

Similarly, if an organization is having problems, it may be worth asking the community, current and past board members, and other organizations what the antecedent events were that led to the current situation. Often others see things that we cannot when we are in or too close to a situation (recall blind spots). Seeking historic knowledge can shed light on a situation. Identifying antecedent events can help identify and clarify previous pitfalls, so they can be avoided.

Working together to predict intended outcomes and unintended outcomes allows a team to plan for possible problems. A board can predict that an intended outcome for adopting a process of giving scholarships to at-risk youth will be to increase the number of at-risk youths who use a program. The unintended outcome may be that there are fewer spots for youth who pay for their spots.

A further unintended consequence may be that as a result of having fewer youth who pay, there may be a loss in revenue; in such a case, the board can make the decision to raise money, increase the number of opportunities, charge more for services, or not offer scholarships. The board will need to think creatively about how to move forward to make sure that altruism does not lead to closed doors.

These are examples of how just considering the various components of the moral imagination process can help an organization predict and plan strategically. The use of the whole process, including all steps, can be used to bring a team to a place where they can use a brainstorming process (like design thinking) to find a creative solution. Once a creative solution has been chosen, the strategic planning moves to setting measurable outcomes to help reach goals.

Afterword

As we have examined the component pieces of moral imagination, there are three points I want to highlight. The first issue is that of generalization. Most of the examples given in this handbook are from the education or not-for-profit field. Please know that this process is not isolated to decision-making in these two realms.

Examining literature in other disciplines, one comes across many models and modes of decision-making. *Harvard Business Review* has "7 Steps to Effective Decision Making" and "The Four Processes of Decision Making," and there are many others to be found with a quick Google search. While there are many examples and articles out there, regardless of the discipline, the terms used to define the process of decision-making are captured in the process and vocabulary of moral imagination. This is not accidental.

Several chapters and hundreds of pages could pinpoint the similarities between this model and others; the reason for landing on moral imagination is that it encompasses all of the parts of the models that have been reviewed and that, in one iteration or another, it has been in existence since the 1700s. The classic nature of this process lends credence to its steps and its outcomes. It also reinforces the idea that moral imagination is a process that works in any context.

Second, it becomes obvious even in the name of the process—*moral imagination*—that imagination is a critical component to successfully making decisions. As long ago as the late 1900s, companies identified creativity as the most important skill employees needed in order to be successful in the twenty-first century.

Two decades into the twenty-first century, the need for creativity is even more obvious. If we must have the capability to solve problems that do not yet exist, the only way to do that is to make sure we possess the mental flexibility and imagination to create and envision solutions. Just like the decision-making process, creativity must be expressly taught in schools.

The easiest place to include creativity for students is in the arts. The arts provide an avenue for students to learn to be creative; literature, theater, painting, music, dance—any of these mediums allow for the express development of creativity. The good news is that the same processes by which we access creativity in the arts can be included in such so-called hard subjects as mathematics and the sciences.

The inclusion of creativity in science and mathematics is crucial to national and global success. I know that sounds trite, but it cannot be stated emphatically enough. As someone who began her academic career in the sciences, I have observed that creativity and art cannot be separated from the sciences. Science, the process of discovery, is inherently creative, and the proposition of hypothesis and use of observation to create predictions is the same process we are discussing in decision-making.

The imaginative is interactively engaged and rooted in problematic conditions. This is to say that extenuating conditions cause humans to use their brains in new ways and try to process information to create something new or find a new answer—to solve a problem. This is science. The process of creating, whether in science or in art, is inherently the same and, as such, we need to foster this process.

In the absence of creative problem-solving, we are creating individuals who will behave as robots, repeating what they are told and having no eye toward futuristic evolutions. Creativity must be fostered and explicitly taught if we are to have citizens who are able to imagine new solutions and realities in all realms of industry.

Finally, increasing creativity in decision-making is the only way to work toward decisions that increase social justice, toward eradicating racism and exclusionary tactics in cultural systems. For this final point, credit must be given to the work of the late Maxine Greene. Greene, who served as philosopher in residence at the Kennedy Center and was a career educator, maintained that the arts were critical to the quest for social justice.

In an oversimplification of connecting the dots, Greene's argument is as follows: we must have the arts to have social justice. The arts in schools support and develop the imagination. As we have seen, the imagination is critical for the development of empathy. In the absence of empathy, individuals do not care enough about those who are "other" to work toward a world where there is only "us."

Writers who begin to write about cats have small connections to the animals—only what their senses tell them about cats. As their imagination and skill develop, they can begin to think creatively about what a cat may be seeing or feeling, they begin to show empathy toward the cat, and their writing will begin to reflect their ability to put themselves in the cat's position.

The arts are crucial because they encourage and build creativity and imaginative capacity. This is necessary, because if one does not have the capacity to imagine what it is like to be a cat, something that has most likely been seen and experienced, it is almost impossible to expect the capacity to imagine what it is like to be someone who is hurting or living in a war-torn area or doesn't have enough food.

Without the development of this capacity, there is a lack of ability to be able to empathize with someone with whom there is no direct connection, someone who lives on the other side of the world. If one cannot put oneself in those shoes, there is less likelihood of helping that person, that other, to find a voice.

The arts are necessary as they set the stage for empathy. I must care about someone else and be able to put myself in that person's shoes in order to work to ensure that that person's rights are preserved. One must imagine the world as one wants it to be and actively work to create it.

One of my real motivations for writing this book is that I believe we can actually move creativity, critical thinking, and problem-solving to the default. If we make these things "common," generations maturing now can expect people to behave this way—to take in information, consider bias, look to new solutions for new problems—rather than have such behavior be the exception. I have hope in people and in the underlying understanding that the best choice is truly in the choice that is in the long-term best interest of us all.

Please reach out to me. I am happy to work with you personally or with your organization to improve your process of increasing the use of imagination in decision-making and in envisioning how to use the tremendous advances around us to create sustainable solutions. I believe firmly in the power of each of us to make a difference. We cannot wait or rely on others to do it for us or legislate it into action. Education, imagination, and creativity will provide innovation and motivation. Keep learning. Keep thinking. Keep imagining.

Appendix

A Brief History of Moral Imagination

> It is a way of seeing and feeling things as they compose an integral whole. It is the large and generous blending of interests at the point where the mind comes in contact with the world. When old and familiar things are made new in experience, there is imagination. When the new is created, the far and strange become the most natural inevitable things in the world.
>
> —John Dewey, *Art as Experience*

As the process of moral imagination is unraveled, a brief historical overview helps illustrate how this process developed and why it can be applicable to any situation. The historic and philosophic bases for this are very clear.

Constructivist philosopher and education reformer John Dewey cautions against the custom of identifying the imaginative, which is interactively engaged and rooted in problematic conditions, with the imaginary, which is subjective (Fesmire, 2003). This is an important point, as problem-solving and creating solutions need to be objective and tied to the components of the situation that one is trying to resolve, rather than subjective and prone to the whim of the person in charge.

It is easy to find examples of this in daily life, the times when solutions have been presented that have nothing to do with solving the problem at hand but rather work to fulfill the whim of the person making the decision. As an example, think of people who have been put into positions for which they were not well suited, because others wanted them in that position—such as a coach playing his son who doesn't throw well as a quarterback or a CEO putting her unqualified daughter in as a district manager.

Roger Scruton reminds us, "Doing something imaginatively involves doing it thoughtfully, where one's thought is not guided by the normal processes of theoretical reasoning, but instead goes beyond the obvious in some more or less creative way" (quoted in Mullin, 2004).

The creative component of moral imagination allows the decision makers to actively imagine a solution that has never been utilized, that may work where something else has not worked. It is the process of utilizing empathy to "put oneself in the other person's shoes" and to consider possible consequences that may result from a given decision. Imagination is not fabrication or fancy, as it is commonly construed, but a "creative reflective activity" (Johnson, 1993). It is not making up facts, but taking things that are known to be true and "ordering or structuring representations in a new manner" (Johnson, 1993).

While this use of imagination for creation of alternative solutions and representations is comfortable and common in art, it is equally pertinent to all disciplines. This process of utilizing the imagination and pairing it with judgment makes it moral. The use of the imagination to create the best possible outcome to a tense situation creates moral imagination. Moral imagination is the process of utilizing imagination to more effectively make moral decisions. It is creative capacity used to engage in futuristic problem-solving. Moral imagination is at once reflective and farsighted: it takes into account antecedent events while looking toward the future to envision the ideal. It takes into consideration the various perspectives of the stakeholders and looks for innovative solutions.

Moral imagination takes this process of imagination and, through the additional consideration of consequences and empathetic review, elevates it to moral. It culminates in a creative solution that considers all stakeholders and puts individuals and organizations in a place to plan strategically to reach the creative solutions. The concept of moral imagination is evident in a vast array of business, political, and social literature. As mentioned in the introduction, the term is used currently in the political arena and, interestingly, has been used by both conservative and liberal camps. It is also used in philosophy, literature, architecture, and religion.

Regardless of the discipline or political leanings of the authors, there are strong central components that emerge as common within these descriptions or characteristics of moral imagination. These components are brought forward and become the key points that create a process that can be followed to make decisions that are morally sound and, because of the extent of the process, can be transparent and easily communicated by decision makers.

Thomas McCullough, in *The Moral Imagination and Public Life*, defines moral imagination as "a capacity to empathize with others and to discern creative possibilities for ethical action. The moral imagination considers an issue in the light of the whole" (quoted in Fesmire, 2003). "It is the application of creative reflection to situations, topics, propositions and emotions that are morally significant" (Mullin, 2004).

David Martinson more clearly identifies the purpose of moral imagination when he states, "If one does not recognize that there is an issue or circumstance in which one has an obligation, it is difficult to take [such] a stand" (Martinson, 2003). John Kekes, in *The Morality of Pluralism*, identifies moral imagination as the "mental exploration of what it would be like to realize particular possibilities" (quoted in Fesmire, 2003).

Kekes also considers the function of moral imagination as to "enlarge the field of our possibilities and correct the mistakes we tend to make in judging what our possibilities are. Thus, through moral imagination we acquire moral breadth and depth. But moral imagination also increases our freedom by increasing both our possibilities and our realism about what they are" (Kekes, 1991).

Moral imagination is the ability to imagine which antecedents created a problem, how the various constituencies involved in the problem may view the events, and how the various consequences and outcomes would unfold. The process of moral imagination in decision-making increases the thoughtfulness of the decision.

Listed in moral development theory as one of the first steps of moral development (Rest, 1979), moral imagination is a concept that permeates many disciplines and, by one name or another, most aspects of our lives. John Kekes, in *Moral Wisdom and Good Lives*, identifies moral imagination as one of the three modes of reflection. He says, "Moral imagination enlarges our fields of possibilities" (Kekes, 1995).

Paul La Forge identifies the need for moral imagination in the ethical process: "Moral imagination was conceived as a three-stage process of ethical development. The first stage is reproductive imagination that involves attaining awareness of the contextual factors that affect perception of a moral problem. The second stage, productive imagination, consists of reframing the problem from different perspectives. The third stage, creative imagination, entails developing morally acceptable alternatives to solve the ethical problem" (LaForge, 2004).

Even further back historically, Adam Smith saw the importance of imagination in making decisions when, in *The Theory of Moral Sentiments* (1759), he described an imaginative process as essential not only to understanding the sentiments of others but also to moral judgment. Sir Edmund Burke is credited with coining the term moral imagination. He references moral imagination in *Reflections on the Revolution* (1790): "All the decent drapery of life is to be rudely torn off. All the super-added ideas, furnished from the wardrobe of a moral imagination, which the heart owns and the understanding ratifies as necessary to cover the defects of our naked shivering nature, and to raise it to dignity in our own estimation, are to be exploded as a ridiculous, absurd, and antiquated fashion" (Burke, 1790).

This definition is clarified in Russell Kirk's interpretation of the work (1971) when he explains, "By it [moral imagination] Burke meant the power of ethical perception which strides beyond the barriers of private experience and events of the moment." This is again a call to see imagination as the process by which we can go beyond what we know and which happens by taking into consideration factors outside of ourselves to come up with new ways to envision what can be.

In other words, Kirk looks at it not just as a way to make better decisions but also as more of an evolutionary obligation to utilize skills that are innately human, as he defines moral imagination in *Enemies of the Permanent Things* (1969): "The moral imagination is the principal possession that man does not share with the beasts. It is man's power to perceive ethical truth, abiding law, in the chaos of many events. Without the moral imagination, man would simply live day-to-day, or rather moment-to-moment, as dogs do. It is a strange faculty—inexplicable if men are assumed to have an animal nature only—of discerning greatness, justice, and order, beyond the bars of appetite and self-interest."

Kirk's moral imagination enabled people to see their lives as part of, in Burke's words, "a partnership not only between those who are living, but between those who are living, those who are dead, and those who are to be born" (quoted in McLemee, 2004). By these definitions moral imagination is once again connected with antecedent events, empathy, and the recognition of long-term consequences.

The idea that the imagination must be cultivated and utilized in an effective decision-making process begins to seem obvious. There is also a historic and pragmatic basis for the components that become the key components of this process of using moral imagination for decision-making.

The most relevant to our changing global society is the idea to look outside of the obvious for a solution; to this end, moral imagination has a unique place in the problem-solving and decision-making lexicon. Moral imagination recognizes antecedents and consequences. It is the ability to creatively reflect on a situation by looking beyond normal and obvious conclusions to find ideas that may not be initially apparent.

Moral imagination is inherently futuristic. The use of imagination requires creating images of what "could be" and therefore involves the consideration of possible consequences. In application, identification of the process of moral imagination should indicate thoughtful decision-making as evidenced by examining antecedents, considering multiple perspectives, and imagining possible consequences of the available outcomes. There are decided points researchers can look toward to determine if moral imagination is being used.

Author and philosopher Stephen Fesmire refers to recurring themes in Dewey's writings as tools for increasing the capacity to morally imagine solutions (Fesmire, 2003). Dewey references two recurring "imaginations": (1) empathetic projection and (2) creatively tapping a situation's possibilities (cited in Fesmire, 2003).

Fesmire further explains empathetic projection as taking the attitudes of others to "stir us beyond numbness so we pause to sort through others' aspirations, interests and worries as our own. Creatively tapping a situation's possibilities refers to overcoming the 'inertia of habit' which can 'override adjustment of past and present, yielding uniformity and routine'" (Fesmire, 2003).

As we take imagination and begin to look at it in terms of a process, it becomes clear that these ideas can be operationalized. The act of using the process of moral imagination when making decisions must also involve considering the viewpoints of others as if they were one's own and looking for creative solutions that will effectively combine the interests of the stake holders.

This process is known as buy-in in trade literature and indicates the acceptance of the decision by those who have to comply with it. The added importance of this process is demonstrated when we examine decision-making literature and see that belief in a solution is more universally important than the actual accuracy of the decision (Hastie, 2001).

Mark Johnson defines moral imagination as "an ability to imaginatively discern various possibilities for acting in a given situation and to envision the potential help and harm that are likely to result from a given action" (Johnson, 1993). Andrew Lau and Richard Devon move this from philosophic to pragmatic when they point out that Johnson's definition involves at least two skills "one being able to imagine many possibilities and their consequences, let's say a creative element, and the other being able to morally evaluate the possibilities, a more rational element (but not purely rational)" (Lau, 2001).

They continue by saying, "Moral imagination is called for by everyone in any situation that is not black and white" (Lau, 2001). Two decades ago, they identified many of "our problems with technology" as the "revenge of unintended consequences. Decisions that appeared B & W [sic] ended up having serious moral consequences" (Lau, 2001). Examples of this range from Edward Snowden to the use of Snapchat in cyberbullying.

Lau and Devon quote Michael Gorman, who broke the process of moral imagination into three steps:

1. Disengaging from and becoming aware of one's situation, understanding the mental model or script dominating that situation, and envisioning possible moral conflicts or dilemmas that might arise in the context or as outcomes of the dominating scheme,
2. The ability to imagine new possibilities, including those that are not context dependent and that might involve another mental model and
3. Evaluating from a moral point of view both the original context and its dominating mental models, and the new possibilities one has envisioned. (Lau, 2001)

Johnson, Gorman, Lau, and Devon's processes, especially those steps that involve creating new "possibilities" and then weighing these possibilities in light of both the old and the new, correlate with John Dewey's theory of imagination and reinforce the importance of imagination and empathy.

"It [imagination] is a way of seeing and feeling things as they compose an integral whole. It is the large and generous blending of interests at the point where the mind comes in contact with the world. When old and familiar things are made new in experience, there is imagination" (Dewey, 1934).

This tie to the pragmatic becomes more important for practitioners and leaders. Moral imagination ties to the practical, when looked at as a process in which we can train leaders and more effectively solve problems. For educational leaders, "the need to be able to inquire and investigate problems with openness and honesty, communicating freely with the parties involved. They need to know how to systematically reflect upon intended actions and likely consequences for the youngsters within their care. Ultimately, their work involves caring for all of the students in their schools" (Enomoto, 2008).

Moral imagination moves from theory to application when its steps are outlined as integral components of effective decision-making.

Books and articles that refer to moral imagination are present in education (Arneback, 2014; Joseph, 2003), business (Werhane, 1998, 1999; Godwin, 2008; Caldwell and Moberg, 2006; Schmidt, 2008), social sciences (Fesmire, 2003; Rest, 1979; Dewey, 1934; Johnson, 1993; McLean and Knowles, 2003), politics (Hühn, 2019; Kirk, 1969; Burke, 1790), health care (Pask, 1997; Jennings and Dawson, 2015), literature (Greene, 1995; Himmelfarb, 2006; Guroian, 1999), engineering and design (Lau, 2001), and art (Dewey, 1939, Greene, 1995, and Martinson, 2003).

The concept of moral imagination appeals broadly to a number of disciplines and researchers. Tools for developing moral imagination include a spectrum of activities ranging from exposure to the arts (Greene, 1995; Guroian, 1999) to meditation (LaForge, 2004). Most contemporary research is focusing on the use of moral imagination to train teachers and nurses and to impact social behavior, both in and out of school and business leadership training (Schmidt, 2008; Godwin, 2008).

Elizabeth Pask published a paper in *Nursing Ethics* about developing moral imagination. In her paper she identifies moral imagination as "a way of seeing" and established a connection between belief and moral imagination (Pask, 1997). Pask draws a set of suggestions for creating compassion and empathy between patients and nurses by encouraging moral imagination. She posits that a predisposition for learning is needed to develop moral imagination, as well as a willingness to share beliefs (Pask, 1997).

In 2006, Gulcimen Yurtsever published "Measuring Moral Imagination," in *Social Behavior and Personality* (Yurtsever, 2006). Yurtsever developed a twenty-nine-item Likert scale that he used to measure moral imagination, which he termed the "Moral Imagination Index."

The results of Yurtsever's study indicate that there is an empirical correlation between moral imagination, personality, and personal value systems. There is a positive correlation between moral imagination, empathy, and comfort with ambiguity (Yurtsever, 2006). Moral imagination negatively correlates with Machiavellian behavior (Yurtsever, 2006). Yurtsever's data lends empirical credibility to the theoretical application of moral imagination and helps support arguments for its inclusion in decision-making and leadership development (Yurtsever, 2006).

Additional studies reflect a continuation of this trend. In 2007, Caldwell and Moberg conducted a study that examined the "antecedents of the process of morally imaginative decision making" and the correlation between moral imagination and the ethical culture of an organization. The purpose of the study was to explore the factors that may engage decision makers in a morally imaginative decision process (Caldwell, 2006).

They were careful to distinguish moral imagination as a process distinct from the actual decision that is made (Caldwell, 2006) and to refer to it as an entity that is "live" in those who use it and "dormant" in those who do not. Caldwell and Moberg identified three characteristics, the evidence of which would indicate the presence of a live moral imagination. First is sensitivity to the moral aspects of a situation, as evidenced by the explicit use of ethics language in dealing with a decision situation infused with underlying ethical issues. Second is taking the perspective of those involved in the decision context; evidence that the subject considered other people's views of the current situation.

The third characteristic of moral imagination for Caldwell and Moberg is the consideration of alternatives beyond the conventional.

Moral imagination is present when a decision maker departs from the official policy framework already in place to handle similar situations. As a measure of a person's cognitive orientation toward moral imagination is moral identity, or the extent to which one refers to oneself in moral terms (Caldwell, 2006).

In this study, participants' written responses were coded on the three dichotomous scales that reflected the nature of moral imagination: (1) the use of ethics language, (2) perspective taking, and (3) the consideration of unconventional alternatives (Caldwell, 2006).

Lindsey Godwin (2008) also searched for empirical evidence to support the use of moral imagination in decision-making. Godwin's study examines the relationship between moral imagination and mutually beneficial decision-making. Godwin demonstrated that individuals who exercise moral imagination, as measured by ability for "developing" and "discerning" are "more likely to generate a mutually beneficial outcome for a situation compared to those who do not exercise moral imagination" (Godwin, 2008).

Pamela Joseph (2003) examines moral imagination in the preparation of teacher education. She identifies elements of moral imagination: perception, rationality, reflection, emotion, and caring for self as integral to teaching education seminars. Lau (2001) reports the need for a morally imaginative approach to engineering and design. Business analyst David Schmidt (2008) calls for a shift in industry to an entrepreneurial moral imagination:

> Business needs to shift its perspective from reactive compliance to proactive moral imagination. Moral imagination is the capacity to discern the bigger picture. It is the kind of imagination that reveals how the web of financial and managerial connections of business is simultaneously a web of ethical interdependencies. The moral imagination lifts our sights from the short-term horizon of our immediate actions to include a wider appreciation of the impact we have over time on diverse constituencies. Most significant, the moral imagination compels us to question the adequacy of conventional wisdom in favor of pioneering new solutions to ethical quandaries. (Schmidt, 2008)

The component parts and effect of moral imagination are further characterized in an article by Moshe Pava (2002). Pava states, "In fact, importing, choosing, inventing, and interpreting constitute the tasks of moral imagination and provide the mechanisms for moral growth" (2002).

As a result of all of these pieces, we can create a cumulative list of characteristics of moral imagination. Moral imagination includes:

- Utilization of imagination to more effectively make decisions
- Ordering and restructuring representations in a new manner
- Utilization of empathy to put oneself in the other's shoes
- Consideration of the possible consequences that may result from any given decision
- Empathy with others
- Ability to discern creative possibilities for ethical action
- Consideration of an issue in the light of a whole
- Application of creative reflection to situations, topics, propositions, and emotions that are morally significant
- Mental exploration of what it would be like to realize particular possibilities
- Enlarging the field of our possibilities
- Predisposition to learning
- Willingness to share our beliefs with others
- Perception, rationality, reflective practice, emotion, and caring for self
- Partnership with those who are living, dead, and yet to be born
- Consideration for antecedent events, empathy, and consequences

Many of these characteristics were consolidated, and the result is the determination that moral imagination in decision-making includes a consideration for antecedent events, empathy, and consequences.

This directly correlates to a partnership between those who are dead, those who are living, and those who will follow; this involves seeing situations as a whole, continuous string of events, not isolated instances. Moral imagination also includes mental exploration to enlarge the field of possible solutions and imagination to create solutions. Finally, individuals who exhibit moral imagination are curious, careful individuals who are open, rational, and reflective.

While it is obvious that moral imagination is beneficial and research has been done to demonstrate that it is effective, there is another reason that it is important to make moral imagination part of the decision-making process. For as much work that has been done on moral imagination, more has been done on effective decision-making. The overlap in terms and key points between effective decision-making and the component parts of moral imagination further support the need to provide leaders and decision makers with this process. Moral imagination involves thoughtful consideration and reflection while making a decision.

Decision-making, in its most basic sense, is the process of choosing. When one makes a decision, one chooses one option over another. It is also true that to avoid making a decision is a choice. Again, according to Hastie and Dawes (2001), a decision in scientific theory is a response to a situation that is composed of three parts:

> (a) More than one possible course of action under consideration . . . (e.g., taking the right or left path at the fork in the road) . . .
> (b) Expectations [formed by the decision maker] concerning future events and outcomes following from each course of action, expectations that are often describe in terms of probabilities or degrees of confidence (e.g., indicating the degree of belief that the right-hand path becomes impassable a kilometer up the trail and that the left-hand path leads to a scenic lake with a good campsite)
> (c) Consequences, associated with the possible outcomes, that can be assessed on an evaluative continuum reflecting personal values and current goals.

Each individual makes hundreds of decisions a day. "Our mind is continually making decisions. There is no conscious activity that occupies the mind than decision making [sic]" (Ressler and Ahrens, 2005). An important point in decision-making theory is that diverse people in very different situations often think about their decisions in the same way (Hastie and Dawes, 2001).

There is a challenge to unite experiences, reasoning, and morality in our decision-making (Ressler and Ahrens, 2005). This challenge cannot be met unless changes in the way decisions are made also take place. Historically, leaders who utilize unique or imaginative problem-solving are viewed as "risky decision makers" (Plax and Rosenfield, 1976).

This is an ironic conclusion based on the fact that this same research characterized individuals who exhibit risky decision-making as persistent, effective in their communication, confident and outgoing, clever and imaginative, aggressive, and efficient and clear-thinking, as well as manipulative and opportunistic. These have come to be known as the characteristics that are now desirable in leaders and decision-makers by progressive companies and organizations—the same organizations that are touting creativity and empathy.

So, while this perception has undoubtedly changed over the decades, it is still evident that individuals in a traditional work environment who utilize creative problem-solving make others uncomfortable. The negative connotations associated with imaginative thinking and the lack of support from directors and peers lead many leaders, who may otherwise be creative, to resort to what Dewey referred to as the "inertia of habit." More directly put: if a leader continues to get criticized for solving problems creatively, the leader may resort to doing things the way they have always been done to avoid conflict.

Management guru Peter Senge (1990) reflects on the process of decision-making and consequences: "We learn best from our experience, but we never directly experience the consequences of many of our most important decisions. . . . We tend to think that cause and effect will be relatively near to one another.

"Thus, when faced with a problem, it is the 'solutions' that are close by that we focus upon. Classically we look to actions that produce improvements in a relatively short time span. However, when viewed in systems terms short-term improvements often involve long-term costs" (Senge, 1990). In Senge's terms, one of the challenges of decision-making is the lack of consideration for long-term consequences.

As Ressler and Ahrens so astutely state, "Good decision-making requires thinking." This thinking needs to include consideration of antecedent events, stakeholder perspectives, how things are interconnected, intended and unintended consequences, and possible alternatives. In essence, good decision-making requires moral imagination.

The effectiveness of a decision equals the quality of the decision times the acceptance of the decision (Ressler and Ahrens, 2005). While, like Hastie and Dawes, many people would be happy to see individuals making rational choices, humans do not make decisions rationally, and even if a sound decision is made, it is not effective unless the acceptance/emotional factor of a decision is high.

Accurately communicating and considering stakeholder opinions with relation to the decision can accomplish high acceptance of a decision. It is also considerably easier to communicate a decision when one knows how one came to a decision, what things were weighed and why the choice was made as it was. This ability to understand how the leader comes to a decision allows the leader to become more transparent.

Research with educational leaders has indicated that most do not have a set way to approach and make complicated decisions. As I visited with college presidents and superintendents, I was amazed to find that they did not always begin the same way when faced with a challenging decision.

When a comparison is made between the problems that occur in making decisions and the solution that lies in the model of moral imagination: the components of good decision-making are captured within moral imagination. It is critical to remember that moral imagination is the process; it is not the act of choosing. A logical conclusion is that if a decision-making process indicates the presence of moral imagination, the decision that follows will have been well considered. Decisions made with moral imagination may avoid many common decision-making problems.

There are central themes to the concept of moral imagination that include empathy, reflection, recognition of antecedent events and consequences, and, when necessary, the desire to create alternative solutions that may bring together oppositional forces. Moral imagination in decision-making includes a consideration for antecedent events, empathy, and consequences. The preceding list of characteristics may be categorized under these topics in the following way:

Antecedent Events	Empathy	Consequences
Ordering and restructuring representations in a new manner	Utilization of empathy to put oneself in the shoes of the "other"	Utilization of imagination to more effectively make decisions
Consideration of an issue, in the light of a whole	Empathy with others	Consideration of the possible consequences that may result from any given decision
Application of creative reflection to situations, topics, propositions, and emotions that are morally significant.	Reflection	Ability to discern creative possibilities for ethical action

Antecedent Events	Empathy	Consequences
Predisposition for learning	Consideration of stakeholders	Mental exploration of what it would be like to realize particular possibilities
Willingness to share one's beliefs with others	Understanding of multiple perspectives	Enlarging the field of our possibilities
Perception, rationality, reflective practice, emotion, and caring for self		Partnership with those who are living, dead, and yet to be born

Consideration for antecedent events, empathy, and consequences

There are certain characteristics or key ideas that are important to moral imagination and decision-making that, while not explicitly outlined above, are important to effective decision-making and implied by the above list. These characteristics include the identification of stakeholders and the identification of personal "blind spots."

As a leader, one who cannot identify one's shortcomings or blind spots will not be mindful of compensating for these deficiencies and will not be able to adequately imagine antecedent or consequential events. Similarly, stakeholders must be identified, or a leader cannot identify who has been affected by a situation in the past and who, as a result of the leader's decisions, will be impacted afterward.

Without understanding our biases and who is affected by our choices, all other discussions of futuristic explorations are moot. A leader cannot compose a creative solution that considers short- and long-term intended and unintended consequences without a full understanding of who and what are involved in the current dilemma.

This brief review of literature should satiate the academics and provide solace to those who need justification. There is a long history that supports these ideas and provides a framework for pulling them into one process that bears the name "moral imagination." There are additional references and evidence that further support the idea that these pieces of moral imagination are the same as those that support best-practice decision-making and decision-making models. Those may be part of a different book for a different day.

References

American Psychological Association. (2001). *Publication Manual of the American Psychological Association*, 5th Edition. Washington, DC: American Psychological Association.

Arneback, E. (2014). "Moral Imagination in Education: A Deweyan Proposal for Teachers Responding to Hate Speech." *Journal of Moral Education* 43(3): 269–281.

Backus, N. and C. Ferraris (2004). "Theory Meets Practice: Using the Potter Box to Teach Business Communication Ethics." *Proceedings of the 2004 Association for Business Communication Annual Convention*, 222–229. Cambridge, MA: Association for Business Communication.

Badaracco, J. (1997). *Defining Moments: When Managers Must Choose Between Right and Right*. Boston, MA: Harvard Business School.

Bass, B. (1974). *Bass' & Stogdill's Handbook of Leadership: Theory, Research and Managerial Applications*, 3rd Edition. New York: The Free Press.

Burke, E. (1790). "Reflections on the Revolution in France." Accessed October 20, 2006. http://oll.libertyfund.org/EBooks/Burke_0005.02.pdf.

Caldwell, D. F. and D. Moberg. (2006). "An Exploratory Investigation of the Effect of Ethical Culture in Activating Moral Imagination." *Journal of Business Ethics* 73: 193–204.

Dewey, J. (1930) "Three Independent Factors in Morals" in *The Essential Dewey, Volume 2: Ethics, Logic, Psychology*, edited by L. A. Hickman and T. M. Alexander. Bloomington and Indianapolis: Indiana University Press.

———. (1934). *Art As Experience*. New York: Perigree Books.

———. (1939). "Theory of Valuations," in *International Encyclopedia of Unified Science*, edited by J. Dewey. Chicago: University of Chicago Press.

Dunbar, S. (2012). "The Cobra Effect." Podcast. *Freakonomics*, retrieved August 9, 2021. http://freakonomics.com/podcast/the-cobra-effect-a-new-freakonomics-radio-podcast/.

Einstein, A. and A. Calaprice et al. (2010). *The Ultimate Quotable Einstein.* Princeton, NJ and Oxfordshire, UK: Princeton University Press and the Hebrew University of Jerusalem.

Enomoto, E. K. (2008). *Leading Through the Quagmire: Ethical Foundations, Critical Methods and Practical Applications for School Leadership.* Lanham, MD: Rowman & Littlefield Education.

Fesmire, S. (2003). *John Dewey and Moral Imagination: Pragmatism in Ethics.* Bloomington and Indianapolis: Indiana University Press.

Geertz, C. (1977). "Found in Translation: On the Social History of the Moral Imagination." *The Georgia Review* 31(4): 788–810.

Godwin, L. N. (2008). "Examining the Impact of Moral Imagination on Organizational Decision Making." PhD diss., Case Western Reserve University.

Greene, M. (1995). *Releasing the Imagination: Essays on Education, the Arts and Social Change.* San Francisco, CA: Jossey-Bass.

Greenfield, W. D. (1991). *Rationale and Methods to Articulate Ethics and Administrator Training*, 332–364. Chicago: American Educational Research Association.

Guroian, V. (1999). "Moral Imagination, Humane Letters and the Renewal of Society." *Heritage Letters* vol. 636. Retrieved August 9, 2021. https://www.heritage.org/political-process/report/moral-imagination-humane-letters-and-the-renewal-society.

Hastie, R. and R. Dawes. (2001). *Rational Choice in an Uncertain World: The Psychology of Judgment and Decision Making.* Thousand Oaks, CA: Sage Publications.

Himmelfarb, G. (2006). *The Moral Imagination: From Edmund Burke to Lionel Trilling.* Chicago: Ivan R. Dee.

Huberman, A. M. (2002). *The Qualitative Researcher's Companion.* Thousand Oaks, CA: Sage Publications.

Hühn, M. P. (2019) "Adam Smith's Philosophy of Science: Economics as Moral Imagination." *Journal of Business Ethics* 155: 1–15. https://doi.org/10.1007/s10551-017-3548-9.

Jennings, B. and A. Dawson (2015). "Solidarity in the Moral Imagination of Bioethics." *The Hasting Center Report* 45(5): 31–38. Accessed March 23, 2020. https://onlinelibrary.wiley.com/doi/full/10.1002/hast.490.

Johnson, M. (1993). *Moral Imagination: Implications of Cognitive Science for Ethics.* Chicago: University of Chicago Press.

Joseph, P. B. (2003). "Teaching about the Moral Classroom: Infusing Moral Imagination into Teacher Education." *Asia-Pacific Journal of Teacher Education* 31: 7–20.

Kekes, J. (1991). "Moral Imagination, Freedom and the Humanities." *American Philosophical Quarterly* 28(2): 101–111.

———. (1995). *Moral Wisdom and Good Lives*. Ithaca, NY: Cornell University Press.

Kidder, R. (1995). *How Good People Make Tough Choices*. New York: William Morrow.

Kirk, R. (1953). *The Conservative Mind: From Burke to Eliot*. Washington, DC: Regenery Publications.

———. (1984) [1969]. *Enemies of the Permanent Things*. LaSalle, IL: Sherwood Sugden & Company.

———. (2014) [1971]. *Eliot and His Age: T. S. Eliot's Moral Imagination in the Twentieth Century*. Wilmington, DE: Intercollegiate Studies Institute Books.

LaForge, P. (2004). "Cultivating Moral Imagination through Meditation." *Journal of Business Ethics* 51(1): 15–29.

Lau, A. (2001). "Moral Imagination," excerpted from "Transformations: Ethics & Design" in *2001 ASEE Annual Conference Proceedings*, edited by A. Lau and R. Devon et al. Albuquerque, NM: American Society for Engineering Education.

Liedtka, J. (2018). "Why Design Thinking Works," *Harvard Business Review*. Accessed January 23, 2020. https://hbr.org/2018/09/why-design-thinking-works.

Marshall, C. (1999). *Designing Qualitative Research*, 3rd Edition. Thousand Oaks, CA: Sage Publications.

Martinson, D. L. (2003). "High School Students and Character Education: It All Starts at Wendy's." *The Clearing House* 77(1): 14–17. DOI: 10.1080/00098650309601222.

Maxey, S. (1988). "Moral Imagination and the Philosophy of School Leadership." *Annual Meeting of the American Education Research Association*. New Orleans, LA: American Education Research Association.

———. (2002). *Ethical School Leadership*. Lanham, MD, and London: Rowman & Littlefield.

McCullough, T. (1991) *The Moral Imagination and Public Life: Raising the Ethical Question*. Chatham, NJ: Chatham House Publishers.

McLean, G. F. and R. Knowles, eds. (2003). *Moral Imagination and Character Development, Volume II: Moral Imagination in Personal Formation and Character Development*. Washington, DC: The Council for Research in Values and Philosophy.

McLemee, S. (2004). "A Conservative of the Old School." *The Chronicles of Higher Education*. Accessed September 20, 2008. https://www.chronicle.com/article/a-conservative-of-the-old-school/.

Mullin, A. (2004). "Moral Defects, Aesthetic Defects and the Imagination." *The Journal of Aesthetics and Art Criticism* 62(3): 249–263.

Smith, D. W. (2003). "Phenomenology." *The Stanford Encyclopedia of Philosophy*. Last modified Dec. 16, 2013. https://plato.stanford.edu/archives/sum2018/entries/phenomenology/.

Parnes, S. J. and A. Meadow (1959). "Effects of 'Brainstorming' Instructions on Creative Problem Solving by Trained and Untrained Subjects." *Journal of Educational Psychology* 50(4): 171–176. https://doi.org/10.1037/h0047223.

Pask, E. (1997). "Developing Moral Imagination and the Influence of Belief." *Nursing Ethics* 4(3): 202–210.

Pava, M. (2002). "Increasing Moral Capital Through Moral Imagination: Its Use for Jewish Ethics in a Time of Crisis." *The Edah Journal: Inquiries into Jewish Ethics* 2(2): 2–11.

Pepper, S. C. (1942). *World Hypotheses.* Berkley: University of California Press.

Pinar, W. F., ed. (1998). *The Passionate Mind of Maxine Greene, "I am . . . not yet."* Bristol, PA: Falmer Press.

Plax, T. G. and L. B. Rosenfeld. (1976). "Correlates of Risky Decision-Making." *Journal of Personality Assessment* 40(4): 413–418. doi: 10.1207/s15327752jpa4004_11.

Ressler, T. and M. Ahrens. (2005). *The Decision-Making Book*. Minneapolis, MN: University of St. Thomas College of Business.

Rest, J. (1979). *Development in Judging Moral Issues*. Minneapolis: University of Minnesota Press.

Schmidt, D. (2008). "The Moral Imagination of Entrepreneurs." Accessed October 4, 2008. http://www.inc.com/resources/leadership/articles/20080101/dschmidt.html.

Senge, P. M. (1990). *The Fifth Discipline: The Art and Practice of the Learning Organization*. New York: Doubleday/Currency.

Snowden, D. and C. Kurtz (2003). "The New Dynamics of Strategy: Sense-Making in a Complex and Complicated World." *IEEE Engineering Management Review* 31: 110–110.

Werhane, P. (1997). *A Note on Moral Imagination.* Charlottesville: University of Virginia, Darden Business Publishing.

———. (1999). *Moral Imagination and Management Decision-Making*. New York: Oxford University Press.

Yurtsever, G. (2006). "Measuring Moral Imagination." *Social Behavior and Personality* 34(3): 205–220.

About the Author

Catherine L. Sommervold is an associate professor and the director of the education doctorate program for Doane University. Dr. Sommervold's work helps students learn to understand, conduct, and communicate about research. Additionally, she enjoys her family, working with local arts and literacy organizations, learning about art and food, hiking, and gardening. Dr. Sommervold's research interests evolve daily but currently focus on decision-making, creativity, and the impact of concussions on college students. Her purpose is to use research and education to encourage people to have hard conversations toward the goal of ensuring equality and individual opportunity. Dr. Sommervold is always interested in collaboration and new ideas, so please feel free to reach out.